PRAISE FOR JEFF O'HARA

AND

HAVE FUN, FIGHT BACK, AND KEEP THE PARTY GOING

"Jeff O'Hara's personal accounting of his journey within the hospitality industry will resonate with New Orleanians since hospitality is the lifeblood of our city. The challenges that he colorfully describes while navigating Hurricane Katrina and the BP oil spill provide an insider's take on those moments in time, and they reflect the resilient attitude that collectively would lift New Orleans up from its knees and ultimately make it better than it has ever been. Entrepreneurs and professionals from all walks of life can learn from O'Hara's experiences and be entertained at the same time."

—Stephen Perry, President and CEO, New Orleans & Company

"A man's life encompasses many twists and turns. Jeff O'Hara takes you on a life's journey few have experienced. From first-time adventures to fame and floods, he relives them all on these pages with wit and wonder. A great road map for any entrepreneur and a not-to-be-missed adventure tale."

—Patti Roscoe, Founder, PRA Destination Management

Paula,
I hope you enjoy this look at New Orleans! Keep the party going!
Jeff O'Hara

"Jeff's is a phenomenal success story that embodies the spirit of the post–Katrina entrepreneurship movement in New Orleans. A witty and enchanting portrait of the day-to-day trials and tribulations of building a growth-oriented business against the backdrop of a city that was simultaneously reinventing itself. This book provides unique insight into how Hurricane Katrina 'made everyone an entrepreneur' and helped weave the spirit into the DNA of a 300-year-old city."

—Jon Atkinson, CEO, The Idea Village

"Jeff's very personal account of his entrepreneurial journey in the face of extreme and unpredictable adversity delivers a refreshing look at the road to small business success."

—Jill Harrington, author of *Uncommon Sense: Shift Your Thinking. Take New Action. Boost Your Sales.*

"Jeff and Allied PRA New Orleans set a high bar in a city that defines hospitality. Jeff has an abundance of the traits he calls upon for his success: charm, persistence, and cajones. We are lucky to call him a partner!

—Steve O'Malley, Division President, Maritz Travel

HAVE FUN, FIGHT BACK,

AND **KEEP** THE

PARTY GOING

LESSONS FROM A NEW ORLEANS ENTREPRENEUR'S
JOURNEY TO THE INC. 5000

JEFF O'HARA

AN INC.
ORIGINAL

An Inc. Original
New York, New York
www.inc.com

Copyright ©2018 Jeff O'Hara

This work is being published under the An Inc. Original imprint by an exclusive arrangement with Inc. Magazine. Inc. Magazine and the Inc. logo are registered trademarks of Mansueto Ventures, LLC. The An Inc. Original logo is a wholly owned trademark of Mansueto Ventures, LLC.

Distributed by River Grove Books

Design and composition by Greenleaf Book Group and Kim Lance
Cover design by Greenleaf Book Group and Kim Lance
New Orleans Photo: ©Shutterstock.com By pisaphotography

Publisher's Cataloging-in-Publication data is available.

Print ISBN: 978-1-7325102-4-1

eBook ISBN: 978-1-7325102-5-8

First Edition

DEDICATION

This book is dedicated to everybody with a dream to start a company—be bold and persist.

It is also dedicated to every person in the hospitality industry whose passion it is to create experiences and provide service to our guests. Sometimes you are the last one up at night taking care of that very last guest or detail, but the work you do creates memories for countless people every day. Thank you for the pride in your work and dedication to the craft.

"I always wanted to experience everything and go down swinging. Well, so far, so good. I know I'm old, but I feel young. And there's one thing they can never take away: Nobody had more fun than I did."

—*Burt Reynolds*
(1936–2018)

CONTENTS

PREFACE

Being an entrepreneur is an amazing journey. The excitement of the unknown, the thrill of major accomplishments, and the control you have over your own destiny are some of the highs of entrepreneurship that cannot be replicated. There have been lots of challenges and setbacks on this journey, sure. I have started ten businesses (so far!), and I have felt the intoxication of success and the heartbreak of unexpected catastrophes. But experiencing the pride of building your business, developing people who believe in your vision, and creating something that brings joy to your customers far outweigh any obstacles you may have to overcome. Besides, if it were easy, anybody could do it!

I am sharing my story for a few reasons. One is because many entrepreneurs will certainly relate to the roller-coaster ride that it has been. Another is because many of the challenges I have had to dig out of on my way have been completely self-inflicted—and frankly, they are funny. I believe Rule Number One for success in life is that you have to be able to laugh at yourself. So while I am laughing at myself, you can laugh at me too!

Finally, having experienced firsthand the aftereffects of Hurricane Katrina and seen the contrast between what was really happening and what was being reported in the global press, I want to share some insights that most people are probably not aware of. These are not the sensational, publicity-grabbing reports that most Katrina books cover. I want to share what real people were doing with their real lives that helped bring a great city and the incentive travel industry back to life.

I hope you laugh, I hope you don't cry, and I hope you will take away a few nuggets from the lessons I have brought forward in these pages.

And if—on the road to entrepreneurship or somewhere else—you are ever standing ankle-deep in sewage on Mardi Gras Day, I hope you think of me.

Jeff O'Hara
December 11, 2018
New Orleans

WAKING UP AFTER HURRICANE KATRINA

"Well, isn't this a fine kettle of fish!"

—RALPH KRAMDEN

Do you want a cup of coffee?" The hand on my shoulder was shaking me awake. It was the last thing I expected to hear. The power had been out for two days, and I was sleeping on a friend's couch. Layton asked again, more firmly, *"Do you want a cup of coffee?"* In my early morning fog, I knew a couple of things: Once I got my senses together, there would be a significant hangover at hand; and second, there was no possible way he could come up with a cup of coffee under these circumstances.

I did know enough that a cup of coffee would be amazing, so I answered, "Sure, but where are you going to get a cup of coffee?" He stormed off toward the back of the house, and I fell back to sleep. A short while later he walked back in and handed me a steaming cup of coffee. I don't know that I have ever received a more welcome gift—before or since. "How did you get coffee?" I asked.

"Dude, I was in the Air Force. It didn't matter if we were in the middle of the desert in Iraq—we didn't do anything until we had coffee."

Given the circumstances, I thought, Layton was going to be a really good friend to have.

How I ended up here on this couch, when almost everyone else had fled New Orleans after Hurricane Katrina, is fairly typical of how a lot of things have come about in my life. Strange situations coupled with a streak of stubbornness and an innate conviction that everything will work out in the end—often intertwined with a complete comedy of errors—explain a lot of what I am about to share with you. My path in life has taken many turns for the better and some for the worse, but do know that never have I felt sorry for myself or my circumstances. I view it all as just one more challenge to overcome. It's been said many times—life ain't for sissies.

CHAPTER ONE

THE HURRICANE: LIVING, DYING, AND THE SEARCH FOR COLD BEER

"When you come out of the storm, you won't be the same person who walked in. That's what this storm's all about."

—HARUKI MURAKAMI

On August 20, 2005, the week before Hurricane Katrina hit, a group of one hundred or so New Orleans hospitality industry folks were gathered at our annual get-together at the Pensacola Beach Hilton. This soirée took place at the end of every summer and was largely an opportunity for us to blow off steam before the busy fall season took hold.

The Pensacola Beach Hilton sits on a pristine white-sand stretch of the Gulf of Mexico, a three-hour drive east of New Orleans. Every year our group of industry professionals—hoteliers, restaurateurs, destination management company representatives, and various suppliers—spent the weekend here under the banner of the Hospitality Education and Networking Association Annual Meeting. Truth be told, there was little if any education, and I suppose "networking" would be a polite description. The group was a lot of the old guard of the hospitality industry, so it was certainly more socializing than business networking. Most everyone had known each other for many years, and there was little on the agenda beyond drinking poolside.

We had seen the developing storm in the Atlantic, and as all New Orleanians do, we kept a wary eye on it. Little did we know at the time that this would be the last time this group would ever be together again in this way. Most of the people in attendance would not be in their same jobs, and some would not even be in their own city by the time it was all said and done. But never mind that—there was a party to be had and nobody was particularly concerned.

A week later, on Saturday night, August 27, I was due to go out with a girl I had recently begun dating, and although the storm was moving toward the Gulf of Mexico, it wasn't a particular topic of conversation. Earlier that day, I had bought some extra beer, wine, and food in case the power went out for longer than usual, and I attempted to get gas. But already there were lines everywhere, and waiting patiently is not my strongpoint. After passing up some overwhelmed gas stations in my neighborhood and downtown, I found a gas station in Central City without a line. It was fairly run-down and the pumps weren't taking credit cards. The neighborhood was sketchy, and I didn't want to be there longer than necessary, so I ran inside and handed the man behind the counter a twenty-dollar bill, put the gas in the tank, and went on with my day. Didn't think much about any of it at the time.

I met Heather, my date, and a few of her friends at Molly's at the Market in the French Quarter. Molly's is a great old dive, run for years by a French Quarter Irish legend, Jim Monaghan. There is an open window to the street at the front of the bar, and Monaghan would sit there and hold court with people on the street and in the bar. There wasn't a single pane of glass in any of the windows or any shutters, because the place never closed. Until he died—and the story of his funeral would take up another book—I don't ever recall not seeing him in that perch. And good old Jim Monaghan is still there, in an urn above the bar.

We went about our evening, starting at Molly's, then hitting some other places in the lower French Quarter and on to listen to music at the Spotted Cat (where the music is always great, and there's normally no cover charge) in the Marigny neighborhood. All of the bars had their usual busy Saturday night crowds, and not once did anyone mention the impending hurricane. Just a normal night on the town. We eventually made our way back to a bar in the Uptown neighborhood where I have lived since 1994, finally calling it a night well past midnight.

The next morning as we tried to sleep, our phones seemed to be ringing off the hook. But we ignored them and lounged around for a while. When we eventually decided to get on with the day, Heather went into the spare bedroom, where her phone was plugged in, to check her messages and came back in a bit of a panic. "Everybody is evacuating the city," she said.

In the thirteen years I had been in New Orleans up to that point, I had experienced dozens of storms threatening somewhere or another in the United States, along with the accompanying discussions and panic that set in even when the threat was minimal. People would discuss hurricanes as a diversion at the office, chattering on about what could happen in the remote chance that the storm would come in—more like capitalizing on an excuse to put off work than actually having any real fears. I thought back to Hurricane Georges in 1998, a Category 4 storm that all the experts predicted would hit New Orleans dead on.[1] Their predictions caused a major evacuation, and when many people went to Mississippi to escape the storm, they ended up being right in its teeth when it changed course, made landfall through Biloxi, and headed quickly north to where many people had evacuated from New Orleans. Therefore, I was not making any rash judgments based on what a weatherman said. Anyone who can maintain a job saying there is a fifty-percent chance something will happen doesn't get much credit from me.

"My father has called five times. He says it is bad!" Heather said. The number of calls was particularly notable since, at the time, her father was a guest of the Federal Prison Camp in Pensacola. I didn't know how many phone calls they were allowed over there, but I presumed he was pushing

---

1   All the experts except one: Nash Roberts. Nash was a legendary weatherman who retired in 1984 but was brought back for special reports when there was an impending storm, up until 2001. The running joke—which was much more fact than folly—was that you didn't worry about the potential of a discussed storm until they dusted Nash off and put him on TV. Nash didn't use Super Doppler or any computer graphics. He had a grease board where he would illustrate the fronts and the pressure systems and predict where the storm would track. With the 1998 storm, he correctly predicted exactly where Georges would make landfall, while everyone else was insisting on a catastrophic landfall on New Orleans. He was roundly criticized by everyone in the media at the time of his prediction but was quickly vindicated.

his limit, and this might be important. I turned on the television, and the first thing I saw was a satellite view of the storm. What had been a relatively meager Category 3 off the coast of Florida the night before had swelled into a massive storm that covered the entire Gulf of Mexico and was a raging Category 5. I am awake now!

Some friends of Heather's were gathering to evacuate somewhere north, and she said she wanted to join them, so we gathered up her stuff, I threw on a pair of shorts and a hat, and we headed out to their house to drop her off. She had invited me to come with them, but the last thing I wanted was to be caught in a massive traffic jam that would surely be what this would turn into (the eighty-mile trip to Baton Rouge reportedly took eight hours). Better to take my chances with the wind and the rain.

The real eye-opening moment occurred as we headed down my street. Fat Harry's is a local hangout that sits on St. Charles Avenue, a few blocks from my house. A good Louisiana boy named Vic LaBorde ran it for many years, and Vic didn't close for hurricanes or floods or snow or riots—nothing. He made mailmen look like pikers. As we turned onto St. Charles Avenue, we saw it: The big wooden doors of Fat Harry's were closed. Tight. Locked shut. I couldn't believe it. I had never imagined such a sight, and I realized quickly that the supplies I had stockpiled were in quantities based on the reliance that the bar would be open. Huh. It took a bit for this to sink in, but I wasn't particularly concerned; I was sure there would be a solution. When I finally got around to checking my voice messages later that day, one of them was from Vic, warning that he was closing and evacuating and inviting me along with him.

No matter, I thought. There were always a lot of folks who thought the same way I did and would be around. I would just figure out who had stayed and take it from there. On the way back from dropping Heather off with her friends, I called a few people, receiving voice mail on the first couple and then reaching my friend Debbie Branham, who answered right away. As it turned out, she had gone to Brownsville, Texas, for the weekend to visit her husband, who was working out of town for a few months. "I am in Texas with Carl," Debbie said, "but Layton is at my house dog sitting, and he has a roast in the oven." Problem solved. I gathered up my supplies of alcohol and headed to Debbie's.

When I arrived at Debbie's, Layton did indeed have a large roast in the oven. I didn't ask why, but this was definitely a good sign. We had a beer from my supply and made small talk, then fed the dogs and decided to go see what was happening in the world. It was warm and humid, typical for August, and becoming a bit overcast from the clouds coming in off the Gulf of Mexico. There was less traffic on the streets than on a normal Sunday, but it was by no means quiet. Some people were clearly packing up to evacuate and others were going about their business as they would any other day.

· · ·

New Orleans has its share of salty female bar owners, and in 2005, Florence "Ms. Mae" Bingham was at the top of the heap. Sporting a mile-high white bouffant hairdo that hadn't changed since the 1950s, an ever-present cigarette, and the vocabulary of a sailor, Ms. Mae was a legend. Her location had moved a couple of times, but her absurdly cheap drink prices never changed. Years back, a friend of mine from New York almost got tossed out of her previous location for arguing with the bartender about the low cost of a round of drinks. Apparently he thought the bartender was making a mistake and that six drinks couldn't possibly cost only eight dollars. At Ms. Mae's they could.

The current iteration of Ms. Mae's lounge is located on the corner of Napoleon Avenue and Magazine Street in my Uptown neighborhood. She moved from a location farther up Magazine to take over a large, if some-what ramshackle, bar called The Club, renaming it as the awkward-sounding and grammatically incorrect Ms. Mae's The Club. Anybody who has ever driven down this stretch of Napoleon Avenue would recognize it by the gigantic "Open 24 Hours" painted on the side of the wall.

So it was no surprise that Ms. Mae's was open, and we spent a good bit of the afternoon and evening lounging around there. A citywide curfew had been put in place, but the hearty souls who were still kicking around New Orleans were unconcerned. Later that night, Debbie called to see how we were doing, and I told her we were at Ms. Mae's. Always the mother figure, she admonished, "There is a curfew on! You should have been home two hours ago! You could get arrested!" I told her we were shooting pool with the National Guard, and they didn't seem at all concerned about the curfew violators in their midst. No consolation to Debbie, but good enough for me.

The bar was in fact quite full with the normal supply of odd characters who frequented Ms. Mae's, some people like us whose usual bar had closed, and a decent-sized contingent of National Guard members who had been called in to protect the city—but who currently had nothing to do. I imagine if the Guard had enforced the curfew and run everybody out, they would have been even more bored than they already were, so they had an incentive to keep us around. As is typical in New Orleans, strangers talked to strangers, and everybody became fast friends, National Guard and all. By midnight, Layton and I had been in the booze for about twelve hours, so we decided to call it a night.

The next morning we awoke to the impending storm. If you have ever been in front of an oncoming hurricane, you know that it has a certain feel and smell that is distinctive. The skies were alternating between gray and somewhat sunny, and it was breezy but not intimidating. If anything, the weather was a welcome respite from the oppressive heat and humidity that August brings to the Gulf South. We sat on Debbie's porch with our coffee and enjoyed the pleasant weather, occasionally going back inside to check the news—but there wasn't much we could do about anything at this point anyway. The latest reports had the storm making landfall to the east, which was very good news. We had an inclination this was coming when the Weather Channel's Jim Cantore moved his live broadcast location from downtown New Orleans to Gulfport, Mississippi.[2]

2   For those who live in areas where weather-related issues are frequent, Jim Cantore is like the proverbial "canary in the coal mine." He is always directly in the teeth of where the worst part of the storm will hit. It is a running joke among regular viewers as to whether Jim is the world's best storm commentator or if he is being punished for some unpublicized Weather Channel transgression. I tend to believe the former, but every time you see him clinging to a telephone pole in hurricane-force winds, pummeling rains, or driving snow, it does make you wonder.

The storm came through later that morning, and by that time, we had segued from coffee to beer. We sat on the porch watching it roll in. I'd been through many storms of every kind, and this one was nowhere near the worst I had experienced. It didn't rain much at all. Occasionally the wind got up to a point where debris was flying around enough to make us go back inside temporarily, but it mostly seemed no worse than any of our daily summer squalls.

After a couple of hours, the storm had passed, and we set out to assess the damage. There were a lot of tree limbs down, so we took Layton's chain saw and some tools and began clearing debris from Debbie's street. Then we loaded up the truck and headed out to see how we could help. We came across several people whose downed tree limbs were blocking their driveways, and we helped them all clear paths out. Heading up St. Charles Avenue, we found lots of debris in the street, so we had to drive up the streetcar tracks to reach Audubon Park. St. Charles has a beautiful canopy of centuries-old oak trees lining the street, and where there are trees, there are limbs. The street was full of them. But we saw no wholesale uprooting of trees here either—just a lot of limbs down. Audubon Park—which was chock-full of trees of every southern variety—looked like a bomb had hit it.

The vast majority of the damage we witnessed was tree limbs—not much in the way of people's homes and property. After a couple of hours of seeing what we could do and satisfied we could do no more, we made our way back to Ms. Mae's. It was mid-afternoon and by then the power had been out for a while, so the beer was warm and there was no ice for cocktails. But everyone was in a good mood, and Ms. Mae was holding court on a barstool outside the front door. Passersby and bar patrons stopped to chat with her. As was typical, she eventually got bored with the conversations and ended them abruptly. Either the bartender or one of the regulars would randomly deliver cigarettes or a beer to her, so she never had to get up. Sort of like serving the queen.

All of the bar's doors were open, providing the only light inside. The bartender had a flashlight so he could dig deep in the cooler. He was keeping tabs on a scrap of paper. But it was pretty busy, so mostly the tabs were on the honor system. You let him know what you had and paid up when you left. The rest of the night passed uneventfully.

. . .

The next day, things started to get a little dicey. We had a transistor radio—leave it to Layton!—and we were listening to WWL-AM, which had continuous coverage of the storm. Reports were starting to come in about some areas of the city that were flooding. That was not particularly unexpected news, given the city's low-lying topography, but still it seemed a little odd, given how little rain had fallen. As the day went on, the number of reports intensified, and people started calling in to the radio station talking about rising waters. I will never forget one exchange with a panicked caller from neighboring Jefferson Parish (a parish in Louisiana is the equivalent of a county everywhere else). The caller was watching the water rise around his house even though the storm had ended over twenty-four hours previously. "The water is rising around my house and I had to move up to the second floor! The storm is long over—what is going on?" The radio host said, "I don't know how to tell you this, but the pump operators were evacuated before the storm by Parish President Aaron Broussard, and all of the pumps are off."

New Orleans and the surrounding communities lie in a basin that is below sea level in many places. Since getting even normal amounts of excess rainwater out of the area requires an uphill journey—all you physics majors out there see the problem here—"drainage" requires a system of underground pipes and pumps to get the water into what are called outfall canals and into Lake Pontchartrain, which forms the northern border of Jefferson and Orleans Parishes. That the parish president would evacuate the pump operators at precisely the time that they would be needed most is beyond comprehension. I sat there, mind-boggled, asking Layton if I had heard that correctly. Surely not. But yes, I had.

Unfortunately, this was simply the first sign of the complete failure of government at every level that was about to become nakedly apparent. Aaron Broussard, the man who ordered the operators' evacuation, did not pay enough for that stroke of idiocy, but he eventually went to prison for unrelated circumstances that involved accepting bribes and putting his mistress on the payroll in a no-work parish job. Karma will get you sooner or later.

As it turned out, the break we received when the storm went east of us was nullified when the winds from the storm came in straight from the north across Lake Pontchartrain.

The lake and the surrounding canals are tidal, and the water eventually flows out to the Gulf of Mexico. But Katrina had churned up a massive storm surge coming in from the Gulf, and now that surge was met by winds blowing straight at the already weakened levees protecting the north and east sides of the area. This ultimately caused them to give way in multiple locations. Thus, long after the storm had passed through, did the now notorious flooding begin to wreak havoc on New Orleans and her surrounding communities.

• • •

It was a while before the cause of the flooding became clear: Cracks were developing in the levees that surround the city and protect it from tidal surges along the lake, the working canals, and the river. The levee system is overseen by a local entity called the Levee Board, but it is ultimately the responsibility of the Army Corps of Engineers. It seems the Levee Board people and their Corps counterparts had a cozy relationship. Whenever mandated inspections were due, the Corps people would fly in and get picked up at the airport by their Levee Board counterparts, take a ride past and over the levees, deem everything in good order, and head off to Galatoire's for a three-martini lunch. Everyone stayed happy and the funds kept flowing.

Unfortunately for our hapless friends at the Levee Board and the Corps (and the innocent residents of the area), the primary point of erosion in an earthen structure that is subject to the flow of water is *below* the surface of the water. Looking at the top of the levee does not give you an idea of the stability of its weakest point. But hey, I like long lunches at Galatoire's too . . .

• • •

Layton's mother was in Baptist Hospital, just a few blocks from my house, and had not been doing well even before the hurricane. The power had been out since the storm hit, and all the emergency generators were on the ground level of the hospital and had flooded out. Gallant teams of doctors and nurses were trying to keep patients comfortable in the stifling heat, but it was a tall order. Layton got a call from his sister at the hospital telling him that their mother was not going to make it. We immediately headed over there. The hospital sits in a particularly low-lying and frequently flooded area of Uptown at the corner of Napoleon and Claiborne Avenues, and the water had suddenly filled in all around it. We drove all around, walked around, and couldn't get anywhere near it. The entire hospital was surrounded by water four to five feet deep. We heard helicopters whirring above our heads. They were evacuating patients from the rooftop a couple at a time.

Then the call came that it was too late; she had passed. We never did get a full autopsy or cause of death, but it is likely the sweltering conditions and general chaos inside the hospital contributed. On September 11, a full two weeks later, forty-five bodies were recovered from Baptist Hospital.

Layton was stone-faced and silent. I had no idea what to say, so I sat there quietly and waited for him to make a move. We just sat in his truck at the edge of the water in silence for who knows how long, and then we headed to Ms. Mae's.

• • •

When we arrived at Ms. Mae's that afternoon, we made an amazing discovery: The beer was cold and the cocktails had ice! Such a miracle to be bestowed on our band of stragglers! Mae was in her usual spot on the side-walk holding court, and I approached her to express my pleasure with our newfound good fortune. "Mae, this is fantastic!" I said. "Where on earth did you come up with all of this ice?" The glare I received in response was worse than any I have ever experienced (and I have probably been glared at more than most people). I slunk away, embarrassed to have asked. I never did get the answer; maybe she'd stolen it from the police department across the street or something.

CHAPTER TWO

THE ESCAPE: COME HELL AND HIGH WATER

"If you are going through hell, keep going."
—WINSTON CHURCHILL

Later that day, as we lazed at Ms. Mae's, we were slowly coming to the realization that our little worry-free world of cocktails and shooting the breeze all afternoon was not going to last forever.

The mayor had come on the radio to say that the power might not be back on for weeks. So our minds turned to when and how we should start thinking about evacuating. It occurred to me that the twenty dollars' worth of gas I purchased the previous Saturday was just about gone, and with the power out in the entire listening area of WWL-AM, the nearest functioning gas station was going to be far away.

I pondered this out loud while a small group of us sipped our beer, and our friend Chris remembered that his sister's wrecked car was parked in front of his house, and there was probably gas in the tank. Layton, being an Air Force mechanic, had no problem showing us how he could use his mouth and a couple of tubes to siphon the gas from the wrecked car into my SUV, and I was the proud owner of a quarter tank of gas! I asked Chris what I could do in exchange, and he asked if I had any pot. Now, I hadn't smoked in over twenty years, but Debbie's sixty-something-year-old husband did, and I remembered seeing a bag in the refrigerator. I swung over to her house, grabbed it, and brought it back for Chris. It was a bizarre Katrina barter system at its best! Everyone was happy.

Earlier in the day, as we passed the A&P grocery store a block from Debbie's house, we saw looters piling out of the store with their arms full. Inexplicably and out of nowhere, Layton decided to swerve into the parking lot at full speed, where he screeched to a stop in front of the store. He jumped out of the car with an industrial flashlight, screaming at the looters to put the things back—and that he was going to arrest them all. (Which he couldn't, of course.) I finally convinced him to get back in the car so we could get out of there for our own safety. We decided to drive to the fire department a few blocks away to tell them what was going on and ask them to radio the police. A group of firemen stood outside, and polite as could be, they informed us that their radios could not communicate with the police department. *What?* First responders are not on the same radio network?

It tragically came to light later that this was a huge problem. The inability of the various emergency agencies to communicate hampered their ability to work together in the rescue efforts. It was just another indication of how royally screwed up this was all about to become. With all the money we pay in taxes, nobody in the entire history of government thought it would be a good idea for the fire department to be able to communicate with the police department in an emergency?

Cell service had long since stopped working, so we drove over to the police department to report the looting. An already overworked officer dismissed our report. "Buddy," he said, "I just found a body floating in the street. You want me to worry about some looting?" It took some doing, but I finally convinced Layton that we couldn't solve this problem ourselves and that our talents would be better utilized at Ms. Mae's.

After pulling off the gas-for-pot barter, I drove over to my house at dusk to pack up some clothes, since Layton and I figured we should think about leaving the next morning. What I found there was shocking. We had driven by the house earlier when reports of flooding began, and it was bone-dry around my house and in the surrounding neighborhood. The closest water had been around the hospital, and that was ten blocks away in an area that often attracts water. But when I returned just hours later, the whole neighborhood was deep in water. I parked a few blocks away on the highest ground I could find and worked my way to my house through chest-deep water. My house is elevated several feet off the ground, so the water hadn't made it inside yet. But it was clearly only a matter of time.[3]

I packed a duffel bag with what I could hold over my head and waded back to my car. I was starting to feel the gravity of the situation, but, in a weird way, I was kind of thankful for the water because I figured it would keep the looters away.

I made it back to Debbie's and told Layton the water was rising fast—we needed to get out immediately. Now remember, we had been at Ms. Mae's all afternoon and were a fair ways past shitfaced, so getting in a car and driving anywhere was the last thing either of us wanted to do at that point. But the alternative was riskier at the moment, given the flood I had just experienced at my house and the regular WWL radio updates about more neighborhoods becoming submerged—seemingly by the minute. I didn't want to go to sleep and wake up surrounded by water and unable to get out. Layton wanted to wait until morning, but when it became clear that I was leaving immediately, he decided to go too. We loaded the dogs in his car and packed up what little food and booze was left. He headed toward Houston to take the dogs to Debbie, and I headed north since I had already made previous plans to meet up with friends from Atlanta the following weekend.

• • •

As it turned out, I had to head south at first, because the only bridge open was the Crescent City Connection going across the Mississippi River to

---

3   For all you physics majors out there, in a flood event like this one, the water flows with gravity to the point of the lowest ground. So even though my house was five feet below sea level, other areas were even lower, and thus, they would flood first, until the water reached the next-lowest level. Kind of like when the tiger approaches and the first guy puts on his running shoes. When the second guy tells him it's a waste of time because he can't outrun the tiger, the first guy says, "I don't have to outrun the tiger. I just have to outrun you." I am often asked why the famous historic sections of the city, particularly the French Quarter and Garden District, did not flood. The reason is that the oldest parts of the city were built on the highest ground. While still below sea level, they are higher than everything else.

what is known as the "Westbank." I guessed correctly that I could head west from there and eventually cross back over the river to catch I-55 north on the west side of Lake Pontchartrain. There were no reports of trouble yet on that bridge, while the Twin Span Bridge to the east and the Causeway Bridge to the north had already been reported knocked out by storm surge.

It is 133 miles from New Orleans to Brookhaven, Mississippi. My circuitous route had added at least twenty miles to that. When I pulled out, my gas reading said I had 110 miles' worth of gas in the tank. I had no idea where the first gas station would be, but surely closer than that, right?

The gas gauge had long since been showing LOW FUEL when I pulled off at the exit at Brookhaven. A policeman a couple of exits back had told me he heard there was a gas station open there. I was practically coasting when I found the station—with a line that seemed a mile long. I was sure I was destined to go dry while waiting in that line. Fate was on my side though, as I eventually made it to my place at the pump. But I was soon in for a surprise: I didn't have any plastic.

Dialing all the way back to my Saturday night date, I remembered what had happened. I had a habit of sticking my credit card in my shirt pocket when I was out in a busy bar—rather than putting it back in my wallet. Both my credit card *and* my debit card were in that shirt pocket—somewhere in my house. I hadn't even thought of them since then, since the power had been out most of the time, and cash (or barter!) was all you could use for payment. It may not have even mattered, as both cards were from a local bank whose computers probably were not functional anyway. I looked in my wallet and found a lone hundred-dollar bill—for all intents and purposes at that point, it was all the money I had to my name. It cost ninety dollars to fill the tank, and I left with ten dollars in my pocket.

I drove as far as I could, until about 2:00 a.m., when I pulled over in a rest area somewhere east of Jackson, Mississippi, to sleep. It was so hot I had to leave the car running to keep the air conditioning on—in spite of the looming gas shortage. Every time I woke up, I turned it off until it got unbearable again. Then I fired the GMC back up.

I awoke at dawn and headed on toward Atlanta to meet friends for our trip to Hilton Head for Labor Day weekend. Pulling off at the first exit that looked like it had anything open, I broke the ten-dollar bill for the biggest cup of coffee they had. Back in the car, I poured what was left of the Jameson I had brought straight into the coffee and drove east. Looking into the rising sun, the gravity of the situation I had left behind finally dawned on me: My adopted and beloved hometown was in shambles, and it seemed there was no relief in sight. I had no idea when or if I would ever be able to return, and I knew that was the same for countless friends and colleagues. The images I was carrying—all the radio reports, the looting, the floating corpse, the death of Layton's mother, wading through chest-high water, and the long drive through the night—were taking a toll. Over and over in my mind, I kept hearing the line from the Warren Zevon song "Lawyers, Guns and Money." The shit has hit the fan. For the first time in thirty years, I began to cry.[4]

---

4   Now, if all of this seems like I was rather reckless and nonchalant, perhaps getting what I deserved—maybe so. But do understand that hurricanes come and hurricanes go. There is always a requisite amount of panic and overreacting, and nine times out of ten nothing comes of it. In fact, nothing major would have come of this if not for the negligent actions of the Levee Board and the Corps of Engineers. So hopefully you can understand why I didn't take more strategic measures in the face of Katrina. Knowing what it all turned into, that decision likely seems a little ridiculous now. But from the inside and at the time, it was a minor calculated risk.

CHAPTER THREE

GROWING UP: NO SILVER PLATTERS

"If short hair and good manners won football games, Army and Navy would play for the National Championship every year."

—BOBBY BOWDEN

I was the oldest child of an alcoholic mother and a workaholic father. As such, neither of them spent a great deal of time parenting, and I became an independent soul at a young age. Couple this with their divorce when I was around eight, and I had to learn how to figure out a lot of things on my own. While not an ideal situation at the time, it certainly was beneficial to my entrepreneurial path: I am not scared of any challenge, and I could and can always think, *I have been through bigger ones than this before.*

My mother's family, the Howards, emigrated from Wales to an area near Pittsburgh just before my grandfather was born. Welsh coal miners all, they found work easily in turn-of-the-century Pittsburgh. My great-grandfather died in a mining accident when Grandad was twelve. Suddenly being the oldest male in the household, Lloyd Howard quit school and went to work in the mines himself. He was able to learn a trade on the side, and he spent most of his career as a successful tool and die maker.

The history on the O'Hara side is a little murkier. Most Irish families who arrived in the United States as a result of the Potato Famine refused to talk about their family history. The reason was part shame and part pain. A lot more people died than emigrated, and the conditions in Ireland were horrible. It was a couple of generations before the nostalgia for the Auld Sod that we have today came about.

My grandfather was one of the few enlisted men in modern history to become a general in the United States Army. He commanded troops in the Pacific during World War II and was highly decorated, including receiving a Silver Star for gallantry during the Battle of Okinawa. He was awarded a Purple Heart as well, but he refused it. One of his men was killed in an action that in hindsight he thought he could have prevented, so he was not going to take any recognition for merely being wounded. After the war, he went on to be commander of the New York National Guard and chief of staff to Governor Nelson Rockefeller. He was charming and the consummate officer—no-nonsense, and a great role model for me. His steely-eyed military portrait hangs in my office, and whenever I need some inspiration, I just look the old General in the eye.

My parents had tried to have children for several years, but after a series of miscarriages they decided to adopt. My sister, Susan, who is two years my junior, and I were both adopted as infants. My brother, David, three and a half years younger than I am, came into the world when my mother actually was able to carry a pregnancy to term. I guess they never stopped trying! Good plan, Dad.

Today my sister is a guidance counselor at a school outside of Fort Lauderdale, Florida, and she and her husband have two sons. My "little" brother is taller, smarter, and better looking than me. The only thing I ever had on him was that I am older, and as we get on in years, that doesn't seem like such a great advantage either. He is a professor of philosophy and ancient Greek at Augustana University in Sioux Falls, South Dakota. His wife is an Episcopal minister and they have three children, two boys and a girl.

My parents separated when I was in second grade and divorced about a year later. Most of my interaction with them for the ensuing ten years had to do with the tug-of-war between divorced parents. Each one spent most of our time together telling us how terrible the other was.

My father was an engineer with IBM and ran projects that were way above the understanding of the average human. He even worked on the Project Mercury space missions. My mother had been volunteering in the library at the Ulster County Jail in Kingston, New York, when my parents divorced, and knowing she needed income, the sheriff created a position for her as rehabilitation director. She oversaw the library, education programs for the inmates, and recreation. She was well respected by both the deputies and the inmates.

At one point in the seventies, the sheriff decided to create a rape squad and include female deputies in it. He came to what today would be an obvious conclusion, that rape victims wouldn't be comfortable describing their experience to male deputies. The one shortcoming to his plan was that there were no female deputies at the Ulster County Sheriff's Department! So he quickly deputized Nancy O'Hara as the first one, providing her with a badge and a gun. She didn't typically carry the gun around unless she was on a case, and it was more of a household joke about our "pistol-packing mama." She quickly became quite well-known in the local law enforcement community, as trailblazers typically do.

We were never really given any kind of an allowance, although my father at one point decided we could do household work for ten cents an hour once our regular chores were done. I managed to pull in a couple of bucks a week during that time. Early on, though, I began finding ways to make some money so I could keep up with other kids whose parents were providing all the bells and whistles of childhood. We lived in a firmly middle-class area of the Hudson Valley, ninety miles north of New York City, with the Catskill Mountains on one side and the Hudson River on the other. While the houses in our neighborhood were quite modest by today's standards, most of them had at least an acre of land. And very long driveways. Every time it snowed, I was up and out shoveling as many driveways as I could to earn extra money. In the summer, I mowed the yards of half the neighborhood. In the fall, I would rake everyone's leaves.

When I turned twelve, I was old enough to pick up the neighborhood newspaper route. I had fifty customers spread out over a five-mile walk. There were no streetside newspaper boxes in those days, and every customer got the paper delivered to their doorstep. I did mention the long driveways . . . The Kingston *Daily Freeman* was an afternoon paper except for Sundays, which meant I delivered it after I finished school for the day. In the winter, it would get dark shortly after we got home from school, which meant I made my trudge in the dark and in the freezing cold. No matter—I was earning money and happy about it. The paper would bill me a discounted rate for the papers they brought to me, and I would collect retail from my customers. It was like running a business on a small scale. I had to do billing, reconciling, customer service, and the actual delivery of the product. A great early lesson!

Growing up, I was the only sports fan in the family, and I really wanted to play sports. But I didn't get much support from home in that area—since picking me up at practices and the like was very inconvenient for my mother. She was in a hurry to get home to her vodka. I still managed to play football in junior high and the first couple of years of high school. However, lacking encouragement and with less than an abundance of speed, I ended up spending more time with the pot smokers than with the athletes.

I got in trouble regularly in school and ran afoul of the law on numerous occasions. One night it was drag racing, another it was driving heavy equipment around a lumberyard in the middle of the night; some other infractions were related to underage drinking and the seemingly brilliant ideas that result from it. We were always looking for mischief and trying to outdo whatever trouble we had previously pulled off. It was doubly complicated for me, because everyone in law enforcement knew my mother and so I was easily recognizable. You would think I would have received some breaks because of this, but it was actually the opposite. The police seemed to think they were helping out my poor single mother by inflicting their punishment on me.

But I picked up another entrepreneurial skill during that time. I discovered that I could buy a twenty-dollar bag of weed and turn it into forty joints that sold in the halls of M.C. Miller Junior High for a dollar each. A one-hundred-percent markup! While most businesses don't carry the level of risk that justifies a hundred-percent markup, the importance of healthy margins has always been front and center in my decision making.

At fifteen, I lied about my age and got a job at the Grand Union grocery store as a stock clerk. It paid quite well—$7.00 an hour to start, when the minimum wage paid by the restaurants and mall retail shops was $3.15. I quickly discovered that you received double time for Sundays and holidays, and I volunteered for all of those shifts. When someone on the night shift called in sick, I would stay and work a double shift into the morning. The night shift commanded an extra couple of bucks an hour, so I volunteered for that as much as they needed me and ultimately landed as a permanent night-shift clerk.

School was not one of my priorities, to say the least. If I needed extra sleep, I would skip class. I thought what school was serving up was really useless information that in no way was preparing me for what I thought I would do in life. But fortunately, I have always had a knack for figuring the system out, whatever the system was. In school, between gaming the system and picking up just enough to get me by, I was never in danger of failing anything.

Midway through my junior year of high school, things had become bad enough on the home front that I moved out. I was admittedly causing trouble, and Mom wasn't handling it well. At the same time, I had come to the realization that I did not like being told what to do. That would become a recurring theme in my life and career.

I had managed to save up, and I bought a car with my earnings from the paper route and the neighbors' yard work. I had a decent enough job, and I rented a room for fifty-five dollars a week from a retired Mafia guy who had moved upstate for the quiet life. He would often share his delicious homemade Italian soup with me. Everything was working out well for six months or so until he found out I had a girl over late one night. He got livid, much to my surprise. We were only watching TV on the couch at the time, but he said he would have none of it under his roof. Good thing he hadn't gotten up at the same time the night before . . . Anyway, not wanting to be held to that standard, I packed up, noting the irony of a man whose business routinely killed people being morally outraged at my female companionship. I didn't have a plan for a place to live at that point, but I did have a lot of friends whose parents liked me (or tolerated me, anyway) and were willing to let me sleep on their couches. I rotated around, so I didn't overstay at any one house. If things didn't work out on any given night, I would sleep in my car at Kingston Point Beach down at the river. I was having a great time raising all kinds of hell and running with fun friends, so none of it particularly concerned me.

Joseph Sabatino James Sorcinelli Jr.—JSJSJR, if you will—sat next to me in Mr. Kennedy's eighth-grade English class. We became fast friends and remain so to this day. I spent a fair amount of time on the Sorcinelli couch, and Mama Rose had gotten wind of what I was doing during the rest of my nights. At one point, she sat me down and said, "Jeffrey, this is ridiculous." She decided she would turn the attic into an apartment and that I would live there. I really wasn't given much of a choice in the matter—with Italian mothers you never are—and I didn't protest because I clearly hadn't come up with any better ideas on my own.

The situation wasn't without its ups and downs though. One summer weekend I went up to Lake George with my girlfriend. When I arrived back at the Sorcinelli house, I was shocked at what I found. The cause, as we found out later, was that an extension cord had been run across the attic from the sewing room under the carpet to provide power to my bedroom. It caught fire the weekend I was away and burned the entire attic and some of the main floor of the house. Everything I owned was lost. It wouldn't be the last time.

The insurance company put a mobile home in the backyard, and Joe and I lived in that while Rose and Mary (Joe's sister) lived in Grandma Nardi's house, which was also on the property. I stayed at their home for over a year, until I left for Florida State, and I will forever be grateful to Mama Rose for looking after me.

• • •

At the start of my senior year, I had gone to my guidance counselor and informed him that by the end of the fall semester, I would have enough credits to graduate and that I intended to do so. He resisted at first, but when I told him about my living situation and that I was working full time on the graveyard shift, he quickly capitulated. I am sure he was a little relieved to have me no longer walking his halls to boot.

By the following summer, I decided it was time to get on with the next stage of life and began applying to colleges. I figured I had burned enough bridges around New York, and so I looked south to Florida. Besides— everybody in New York moves to Florida sooner or later! I thought that life on the beach with an umbrella drink sounded like a great relief from New York winters. I was accepted to the University of South Florida and Florida State University, more on the strength of my SAT scores than my grades. At first I planned to go to USF because it was in Tampa, a much bigger city than Tallahassee. But one of the guys I worked with at the Grand Union had been admitted to the architecture school at Florida A&M in Tallahassee, so I decided to go to Florida State, figuring I would know at least one person in town.

That turned out to be one of the best decisions I ever made. Everybody thought I was on the right track. Well, except for one person. A couple of weeks after arriving in Tallahassee and starting school, I received a letter from my probation officer. It stated that I was in violation of my probation for leaving the state and subject to immediate arrest and extradition to New York. Whoops, I thought I had told him but perhaps it had slipped my mind. In the end, reason carried the day, and once I explained and he saw that I was working to better myself, he petitioned the courts to end my probation. As usual in my life, a dark situation sorted itself out, adding to my confidence that this would always be the case. Crisis averted!

I settled in and made friends quickly. Despite being of an anti-fraternity mind-set when I arrived on campus, I found some kindred spirits in the men of Phi Kappa Tau, and I joined during my first semester. It was a diverse group, to say the least. We had some really good athletes, some serious party animals, a handful of studious guys, and a large dose of hell-raisers. We had a lot of fun, but this group of guys also provided a lot of support to each other, and that was quite helpful to me, being in a brand-new and very different environment.

Garth Murphy was an Irishman from western New York. We became roommates and worked together at a local watering hole called the North Monroe Deli. British Steve Hortin took ten years to graduate. Mark "Squid" Cechman was a retired Navy guy who preferred to walk down the hall to the shower and back stark naked (except for his prescription swim goggles). Eric "Link" Praether was a stud basketball player whose nickname drew from the missing link of evolution. Tim "Shotgun" Pickles had a gun for an arm and starred on our football and softball teams. CC, Gonzo, Willie Weitekamp, Pooch Bender, Jim "Leghairs" Lebherz, Mike David—the list goes on and on. We also had Tim Brown (but not the Heisman Trophy winner), Fidel Castro (but not the Cuban dictator), and Paul Allen (a great guy, but alas not the founder of Microsoft). Most of these guys ended up being doctors, lawyers, and Indian chiefs, but nobody would have predicted it back then. Many of them are still close friends of mine—thirty years later.

Once I got past the first few semesters of required courses, I began taking classes in the College of Business and finally discovered that class-work could be interesting. I chose to major in hospitality administration because it was part of the business school and because hospitality jobs seemed like ones that would not keep you tied to a desk.

The first fourteen years of my academic exposure had been focused on subjects that I couldn't see having any relevance to real life. I recall an argument with my tenth-grade English teacher that pretty well summed it up. There was a question on a test that asked what I thought Shakespeare meant by a certain passage. Since it asked what I thought Shakespeare meant, then whatever I thought he meant should have been a correct answer. But the teacher had a different thought about what he meant, and when she graded the paper, she marked my answer wrong. Shakespeare had been dead for four hundred years, so she didn't have any more insight than I did, and by definition, it was an opinion question, so whatever my opinion was had to be correct. Another of my frequent trips to the principal's office ensued. I really had no use for school, but I did know I needed it to reach my ultimate goals, so I kept at it.

Once I got to the college courses in my major, the whole world changed for me. This was *interesting*! And applicable to what I wanted to do with my life. I suddenly became a great student, making the dean's list every semester and even carding a 4.0 once. Why does it take that long to get to coursework that is relevant? In the United Kingdom, students in middle and high school can choose curriculum paths that are geared toward their interests. Without professing to know too much about it, this seems like a much better system than cramming poetry and algebra down the throats of America's next business leaders.

I have stayed close to Florida State throughout my career and doing so has brought me many rewards—mostly due to my relationship with Joe West. An Irishman from South Florida, Joe spent twenty-two years in the Navy. He served as a combat medic attached to the Marines in Vietnam, then transitioned into Navy food service, then went into running restaurants when he retired from the Navy. He arrived at FSU as a newly divorced, newly minted PhD, as a professor in our hospitality department. Dr. West taught Advanced Food Service, which is the last class you take before graduating. That class produced the Little Dinner Series, which was subscribed to mostly by Tallahassee blue bloods—and always had a long waiting list. We served them a seven-course themed dinner every Thursday night. Each week, whatever team we were on served in a different role. You would work as a server or in food prep, sanitation, or management. On the week your team was management, you designed the menu (our theme was Greece), selected the recipes, chose the decor, and directed the rest of the teams in the operation. It was very successful, especially considering that we only had a $200 budget to work with. The guests were always happy, and I suppose they cut us more slack than they would have at a real restaurant—but the price didn't leave much room for complaint either.

Most seniors didn't have class on Friday, so Joe would hold court after class with all who were interested at the Flamingo Café, a popular watering hole just off campus. From those days, Joe and I developed a lifelong friendship. When he became chairman of the hospitality department, he recruited me to join the board of directors of the alumni association and included me in many great events at the school.

• • •

I was involved in a lot of extracurricular activities at Florida State, and this was when I began to realize that I had some leadership skills. I was president of the fraternity and vice president of the Hospitality Honor Society (I know—honor society—*me*??). I played intramural sports and worked bar and restaurant jobs throughout. Juggling all of this and having success in all of it—while rarely missing a party—allowed me to master the time-management skills that are essential to success in business. I would argue that these skills are essential to success in life in general, but as so many people lack them and still manage to stay alive, it makes me wonder.

One day at a lunch with the honor society officers, I met someone who changed the path of my career: Executive VP of Human Resources, Roger Senter of Sheraton (ITT Sheraton at the time). Sheraton hadn't recruited on our campus, but Mr. Senter was there to cultivate a relationship with the school, and Professor Bob Brymer arranged a lunch with him. I had several job offers already, since the hospitality department had a one-hundred-dred-percent placement record, and I had just made up my mind to accept a position in Hyatt's management training program. But it just so happened that I sat next to Mr. Senter at lunch, and toward the end of the meal he asked me what I planned to do after graduation. I told him I had just decided to take the Hyatt offer. He asked me why, and when I told him, he informed me that Sheraton could offer many of the same things. "Don't take the Hyatt offer until you come to Boston to meet with me," he instructed. A free trip to Boston—what could that hurt? Sure enough, the next day his secretary called and sent plane tickets. I was in Boston on

Monday. I received a VIP reception at the Sheraton Boston, including a huge amenity basket in my room. I spent some time with Mr. Senter and other members of the senior management at 60 State Street, and capped the day with a visit with John Kapioltas, the *president* of ITT Sheraton.

I still am not sure what I did during that lunch, but I must have made an impression! Sheraton followed quickly with a job offer that was for a couple of thousand dollars more than Hyatt and the opportunity to pick where I wanted to start out. Beyond all of that, I figured I had the attention of the people at the highest level of the company, and I knew those would be good connections down the road, so I quickly accepted. Just after the first of the year, I was off to the Sheraton Bal Harbour in Miami Beach to start my corporate career in the management training program of Sheraton Hotels.

CHAPTER FOUR

THE NEW ENTREPRENEUR: TURNS OUT I REALLY DON'T LIKE BEING TOLD WHAT TO DO

"If you come to a fork in the road, take it."

—YOGI BERRA

I was excited to start my first real job. I was brimming with confidence and knew I would be a success with this company. The training program was a year long, with nine months spent rotating through all the departments and three months in your area of concentration, which for me was Front Office. It was a solid program and the hotel exposed me to some high-profile events. Sporting events hosted by the hotel included the Super Bowl, the Breeders' Cup, and the Orange Bowl National Championship Game. The Colorado Buffaloes were playing in that game and so for a week, the 1,200-pound Ralphie the Buffalo was stationed right outside our front door. We also hosted live location shoots for some popular television shows of the time, including *Superstars* and *The Sally Jesse Raphael Show*. I made some good friends in Miami, and a number of my friends from FSU settled in the Miami/Fort Lauderdale area. But, frankly, Miami is no place for a young gringo with no money—I was neither rich and white, nor poor and Latino, the two major social groups in the city. I do have great memories of sitting at the Clevelander bar on weekend afternoons. The bar was open to the street overlooking South Beach and was an old-school South Beach dive. Beer was a buck and a half at most, and the people-watching was phenomenal. The combination of beautiful people in skimpy clothes, aging hippies, and various down-and-out hucksters was brilliant. Oh, how that neighborhood has changed now!

Once the training program concluded, I was asked what my preferred next destination would be. It was typical in the hotel business to move every two years or so in order to be promoted. Excited for the next step, I identified Boston, Chicago, San Diego, and Seattle as robust cities where we had large corporately managed hotels, and I listed them as my preference.

My preferences notwithstanding, shortly thereafter, I was informed by our HR director that there was a position in Baltimore that they wanted me to interview for. I had never been to Baltimore and knew nothing about it other than its sports teams. One week later, I was on a plane to Baltimore for an interview, and two weeks after that, the movers arrived to pack me up for the move north. You just didn't turn down an opportunity, because if you did, the next one might be a long time coming.

I was transferred to the Sheraton Inner Harbor in Baltimore as assistant front office manager. Baltimore was a fast-growing tourist town featuring shops and restaurants along the harbor and a first-of-its-kind aquarium, the renowned National Aquarium. The city has a fascinating history dating back to the Revolutionary War. Notably, Francis Scott Key wrote "The Star-Spangled Banner" as he looked out at Fort McHenry during the Battle of Baltimore in the War of 1812. Babe Ruth was born in Baltimore; Edgar Allen Poe is buried there. With all of this, the city has decidedly blue-collar roots, and it was easy to make friends. The people were welcoming and fun. I spent lots of Friday evenings in friends' backyards enjoying crab boils and conversation.

After two years in Baltimore, it was time to look toward my next career step. Once again, I was asked where I would like to go, and, once again, I answered Boston, Chicago, San Diego, Seattle. But time passed, and I was advised by our HR director that there was a position open in New Orleans they would like me to interview for. I had been to New Orleans twice, but as a college student, my exposure was limited to Bourbon Street. I knew nothing else about the city. Nevertheless, you didn't turn down an opportunity at that stage of a career, so off I went.

In April of 1992, in the middle of Jazz Fest, I was transferred to the Sheraton New Orleans as Revenue Manager. At this point, I had lived in four cities in the previous seven years, and each time it took a little while to get my footing and find my social group. But not in New Orleans! My first day on the job, I was walking through the executive floor when someone stopped me and said, "Hey, you are the new guy who just transferred in, right?" I said I was and she said, "Well, new guy, meet us at the Jimani after work, and I will introduce you around."

The Jimani is a great French Quarter dive bar (about a block from where the Sheraton is on Canal Street) that is frequented by many of the employees of the surrounding hotels. It was owned by a great couple from Chicago. Jim Massacci and his wife—known by everyone as "Mom"— were ever-present at the end of the bar. I showed up there at five thirty as directed, and wouldn't you know there were twenty people there to meet me! Everyone wanted to welcome the "new guy" to New Orleans and ask how they could help with the transition. I could see right away that the people of New Orleans are different. They are the number one factor that has kept me rooted here all of these years.

At the time, I was told I would be there two years, and then I would move on to another position in another city. That was the price you paid for quick advancement, and I actually liked that part of the opportunity. You could see a lot of new things and meet new people on the company dime. As it turned out, in two years I was promoted to Director of Front Office Operations, and so I was on track to stay two more years in a city I was really starting to love.

The New Orleans that tourists see is just a small part of the experience of living here. The people are friendly, the food is amazing, the party never stops, and everybody just rolls with it. The people are the differentiating factor here. A friend said it best when he toasted a group of out-of-towners at my 50th birthday party—"In most cities, people have to find a reason to like you in order to welcome you; in New Orleans you are welcome until we find a reason not to like you." It's like the old Irish saying, *There are no strangers, just friends we haven't met.*

At the Sheraton New Orleans, I had the good fortune to work under the leadership of Bob Foster, our General Manager. Bob had been an Air Force fighter pilot in Vietnam, and he demanded military precision. This ruffled the feathers of a lot of people, but I respected it. He would get in at five in the morning and walk the "back of the house," which is hotel lingo for the service staging areas that guests never see but where employees spend most of their time. He believed that if we didn't take pride in the back of the house, we would never take full pride in the front of the house, the guest-facing areas. It reminded me of my grandfather doing military white-glove checks along the top of the doorframes, looking for dust. The point is that if you overlook one detail, you would overlook others.

Before anybody else was even out of bed, he was setting the marching orders for the day. Bob accepted no excuses, and he did not suffer fools lightly. I liked that, since in a hotel of that size—1,100 rooms—there were a lot of factions, and people were always playing CYA. Bob saw straight through it, thankfully. He could spot BS a mile away. As demanding as he was, he respected and rewarded—in his own way—the people who did a good job and hit their goals. While he was known to make us feel very uncomfortable when he saw a line at the front desk, he was by no means a micromanager.

He would sit down with his leadership team at the beginning of each quarter, discuss our goals for the upcoming quarter, and review them at the end of the quarter. I regularly exceeded mine, and he wasn't overly concerned about the details of how I got there. He was only interested in the results. I loved working for him for that reason. He was also a huge proponent of continuing education. He regularly brought speakers in to talk to our team. I remember Ken Blanchard, the author of *The One Minute Manager*, coming in when he was at the height of his popularity. Blanchard was not an inexpensive get, but Bob believed in developing his team. He fully supported me when I asked to take part in the Executive MBA program at Tulane, as he had for our Director of Sales, Mark Wilson, before me. Bob was very well respected in the company and the community. He had made a comfortable life for himself in New Orleans and was prominent in many industry and civic organizations. But when the company opened a brand-new 1,300-room convention hotel, beautifully placed on the Chicago River, Bob was off to be the GM of the Sheraton Chicago. Giving people the ability to own their responsibilities and driving home the importance of continuing education for my team are two things that I fiercely believe in, and both of those beliefs came straight from the leadership of Robert Foster.

Bob's replacement came from Hong Kong—an American named Henderson who had been working in Asia for many years. I can't remember his first name. Doesn't matter, he was an idiot. As far as delegating and accountability, he was 180 degrees different from Bob. I remember one of the first times I realized he was going to be a problem. He was all over me one day: "The telephone operators said you didn't have enough bellmen on this morning." *Really? The telephone operators understand the complexity of bellman budgeting and scheduling? And you would take that as truth without even asking me my view?* This was going to be different, for sure.

Another time, we were in a long staff meeting (I hate meetings, and corporate life is full of them) when I excused myself. It was the Friday before Mardi Gras, we had eight hundred guests arriving, and I intended to help my staff take care of everything that needed to be done. He said (in front of a whole roomful of hotel managers), "Well, someday Jeff will be able to stay in a meeting, and his department will still run." The truth was that I had plenty of management and staff on duty, and my department most certainly would have run on its own. But on one of the busiest days of the year, I wanted to be there in the trenches to help out, provide support, buy them lunch, and do everything I could to make their stressful jobs easier. That's what leaders do.

A NOTE ABOUT MEETINGS

Much has been written about how much time is wasted in meetings and how everyone hates them. Yet they still persist. A Boston Consulting

continued

Group report states: "Managers in the most complex organizations now spend 30 to 60 percent of their time in meetings and 40 percent of their time writing reports (generally used for meetings)." *Are you kidding me? Is any real work being done by these people, and how much overhead is being spent on these salaries?*

To every entrepreneur, I say, "Minimize your overhead." It is one of my most important recommendations, and all these meetings certainly fly in the face of that. The vast majority of the time in meetings in corporate environments is taken up by people bloviating their own agenda in order to get in front of their leaders—rather than trying to advance the goal of the meeting itself.

One trick I find useful—when necessary—is when I call for a "thirty-second rule." If you do not get your point across in thirty seconds, anyone in the meeting can call "thirty seconds" to make you wrap up. Time yourself sometime speaking for thirty seconds; it is actually a fair amount of time. By establishing a rule around time, it takes away the personal aspect of calling someone out.

And even go one step further: Minimize the length of your meetings to start with, so people can spend time doing the things they enjoy about their work and advance the goals of the company at the same time.

Back to the new guy and the Sheraton.

We had three key metrics that our goals were based on—the Guest Satisfaction Index, the Employee Satisfaction Index, and Profitability. I consistently had the highest guest satisfaction and employee satisfaction scores in the hotel, and I always made my numbers. So by any objective measure, I was performing at a high level. I loved my job, I loved the people I worked with, and I loved the challenge of the environment of the hotel business: No two days are ever the same. I envisioned a long-term career with Sheraton, and I told my bosses in reviews that my goal was to be president of the company one day. I regularly put in seventy- to eighty-hour weeks and enjoyed every minute of it. That all changed with the arrival of Henderson.

There wasn't one specific incident that triggered it. There were several. He was just the way he was, and I was the first to get fed up with it. At one point, he told me that he couldn't understand why I had gone for an MBA; that nobody in the hotel business needs one. He asked me why I had wasted both my own and the company's time. Then he sent me off to Atlanta for an aptitude test, ostensibly to evaluate me for promotion, but his assistant told me he was looking for some psychological fault he could use against me. No matter: I came out of the test with flying colors and the highest recommendations.

Again, I don't remember the exact instance that put me over the edge, but I do remember it was a Friday. I was so angry that I could have quit on the spot, but in an effort to keep my Irish temper in check, I made a deal with myself that if I was still mad on Monday, I could quit then. I woke up Monday steaming, and I couldn't get my resignation letter in fast enough. I walked straight out the door that day without any idea of what the future would hold. I just knew that whatever it held did not involve that fool.

Both my mother and my girlfriend were incredulous at my action. They both came from family histories where people worked one job their whole life. When I quit with no next step predetermined, it made no sense to either of them, to say the least.

For me it was a relief. As mad as I was, I didn't realize how much it all was bothering me until I walked out. In spite of having no savings, no job, and no idea what would come next, I felt good about the decision and myself. It was time to head to the bar and let the world take its course!

THE MOMENT WHEN YOU KNOW

Every entrepreneur has a moment like this—when they decide the time has come to take the leap and cut the comfortable ties to a regular paycheck. And most entrepreneurs have considerable chutzpah—or as my

continued

mother used to say, "You sure have brass balls, young man!" (It was not a compliment at the time.) But the people around them may not share the same confidence in the entrepreneurial dream. When I counsel aspiring entrepreneurs, this is one of the things I drive home to them.

If you have a family, you have to set the expectations in advance as to what the possible outcomes could be. It's easy to talk to your spouse about how you could make amazing amounts of money when whatever it is hits it big, but the reality is that there will be many times when you don't have a paycheck, are working twenty-three hours a day, or are under significant stress from any number of things at the company. If you set up these expectations from the beginning and have a plan to implement them together, as a family, when the time comes, you will be going a long way toward maintaining your relationship. Owning a business is hard enough; you don't want to stress your family in the process. Set your expectations and make a plan in advance of the adverse situations, because they *will* happen.

As part of this process, I came to the realization that I really don't like being told what to do. It's why I left home in high school and why at thirty I left the corporate world. There are a lot of idiots in the world, and one of the reasons I became an entrepreneur was to separate myself from them. In the office anyway.

• • •

My first entrepreneurial step was a bit of a misstep, but it had some positive outcomes. There was a company at the time that specialized in getting hotel rooms for people during busy periods in the city. I met one of the owners through work and we became friends, golfing, traveling, and socializing together. He had already taken on a partner to expand to other markets, and knowing that I was originally from New York, he offered to bring me in as a partner to handle expansion in the Northeast. At the end of the day, it was not a partnership. He founded the company, and it was his company regardless of my so-called partner status. When we parted ways, he screwed me financially, which he did to a lot of people during his career. His sister did his legal work for free, so anyone who tried to sue him ended up having to hire an attorney for a prolonged battle, as opposed to having a free lawyer, and eventually, the legal expenses just wore people down. I saw him a few years back in a bar in the suburbs, and he looked scraggly, overweight, and unhappy. Karma is a bitch. Treating people the right way opens so many doors and closes few.

A friend of mine had a similar experience recently with a business he was officially a partner in, but which was dominated by the founder. The lesson here is to make sure everything is solidly in writing, including a clause with some severance or breakup fee if things don't work out.

However, while I was still working there, my brain was in overdrive thinking about how I could further expand my entrepreneurial empire. By leaving Sheraton in the fashion I did, I knew I had the cajones to go after anything. When I was at Tulane, one of my favorite courses was an entrepreneurism class taught by John Elstrott. Our capstone project was to create a new business and write a business plan for it. I had found a building for sale outside of the French Quarter and written a plan to convert it into a small hotel. In my mind, I always knew that I wanted to someday own my business, and this class gave me the tools and the idea that it could actually be done.

Another of the owners had parlayed his success at the company into first opening a bed-and-breakfast and then a small hotel across the street from our office. I decided I could do the same thing, starting with opening a small B&B and working my way up to owning a large hotel. So I dusted off the business plan from Elstrott's class and bought a 5,000-square-foot 1885 Greek Revival mansion at 1216 Louisiana Avenue in the Garden District. It had a beautiful exterior structure but needed some attention inside and to the infrastructure to make it a functioning bed-and-breakfast—not least of which was installing bathrooms in all of the guest rooms. I cashed in my 401(k) from Sheraton and used that for the down payment and the initial working capital needs, and in less than a year, I opened the doors of a five-room bed-and-breakfast, Chateau Louisiane.

For the first couple of years I did everything myself—I made breakfast, I cleaned the rooms, and I greeted the guests. Could I have hired someone to do some of these things? Possibly, but then I would not have had the money to make my next investment. Needless to say, I did not have long discussions with my friends about cleaning toilets, but I was determined to make it on my own and that was what needed to be done. I have a friend who owns a large plumbing company and is a millionaire many times over. And I am sure he plunged his share of toilets back in the day.

Everyone sees the successful entrepreneur as a person at the top, but everyone who made it to the top had to clean a toilet along the way. Those people who stick with their dreams in spite of the mess are the ones who achieve success in the long run.

THE LIFE OF AN ENTREPRENEUR

I had been dating Shawne for a number of years when I decided to buy the B&B, and we moved into the second floor of the building. She thought it was a great idea and was eager to show off the beautiful property and entertain in the grand space. After a couple of years, she found it not such a great idea, and this, coupled with a few other things, had caused the relationship to deteriorate. So it wasn't a gigantic surprise when I returned home from a trip to discover she had moved out. And when I say moved out, I mean she moved *everything* out.

Well, everything except for Pyewacket. Pyewacket was a three-hundred-dollar white Persian cat that Shawne had insisted on acquiring as a kitten. The cat was about as antisocial and disdainful as could be, but Shawne liked her. You know the saying: *To dogs, people are family; to cats, people are staff.* Well, this one had all that attitude and more. When

I returned home, all the furniture had been removed from our apartment, and sitting in the middle of the floor looking up at me with a look of "WTF, idiot?" was that damn cat. Apparently the new apartment didn't take pets, so in a final add of insult to injury, I had no furniture and a cat that had no use for me. And she was seriously pissed at me for losing the furniture. You know those times when you just have to shrug your shoulders and laugh at yourself? This was one of those times.

• • •

Rob Hailey was the director of the Executive MBA program at Tulane, which had started international partnerships with universities in Latin America and the Far East. Students who enrolled in these programs would end up getting a joint MBA from their local university and Tulane, which was quite prestigious in these countries. As part of the program, the students would come to Tulane for classes for three weeks and then the Tulane EMBA students would also go to one of these universities for one week at the end of the program. I had started handling some of the travel for these groups when I was at my previous company, and it was a nice account. I figured that Rob would have kept working with them after I left, since they had the infrastructure in place. But I brought in that business and it was my baby, so it bothered me that I would lose it when I left. I admit I was scared to make the call to Rob, but I had nothing to lose. I called him up and explained that I had left the company but was still interested in managing his groups. I held my breath, but it turned out I didn't have to hold it for long. I will never forget his response. "Jeff, I am working with you, not any company. Wherever you are, I will work with you." Personal relationships are everything in this world, and some people are better at honoring them than others.

That conversation was a big lesson for me. On top of that, Rob and Tulane were the first clients for what ultimately became my Inc. 5000 company, AlliedPRA New Orleans. I will be forever grateful for that. Rob is a good friend to this day, and I see him regularly at Tulane events.

After Chateau Louisiane had been open for two years, I was approached by a mortgage banker friend of mine with an opportunity to buy a second B&B at 1244 Esplanade Avenue, just outside the French Quarter. The B&B had ten rooms and was already nicely profitable. It was an Italianate-style mansion on the Esplanade Ridge. When the French Quarter became crowded in the 1800s, rich Anglos moved up to the Garden District and rich Creoles moved to Esplanade Ridge, both groups building grand houses. It was during that Creole migration a few blocks from the back of the French Quarter that this property was built.

We were concerned that we didn't have any money, but Neal Clark, the mortgage banker, worked that all out—with a combination of an SBA loan, owner sub-financing, and a bit of smoke and mirrors. When all was said and done, Neal and I bought the Maison Esplanade for $900,000. It had a clientele that paid more and expected less than at the Garden District property, so we were able to keep it churning along and making money without a lot of trouble.

I now had three businesses running, and things were going fairly well. The late nineties were a boom time in the industry and the nation as a whole. New Orleans was no different. There was a lot of buzz around the dot-com explosion and the crazy valuations that were being placed on Internet companies. "Hey," they said, "this time it is different." Lots of dot-com people stayed at my B&Bs and bought rooms through my reservation service, so it was all fine with me. I still didn't buy any of their stock, though.

During this time, Neal and I were approached by the branch manager of our bank about a customer who had a 19,000-square-foot historic property at 4228 St. Charles Avenue that he wanted to sell. It would be a perfect conversion to a bed-and-breakfast. The asking price was $650,000, and the owner was in poor health and motivated. We couldn't resist taking a look.

Things got interesting really quickly. The house had been designed by Thomas Sully, one of the most noted architects in the history of New Orleans, and completed in 1892. But more interesting was the fact that the property was notorious in this blue-blood section of St. Charles Avenue. Originally a grand mansion on a grand avenue, it had fallen into disrepair at the hands of some eccentric owners. The owner we were purchasing the property from had inherited it from his mother, who was known as "The Cat Lady of St. Charles Avenue." (You can see where this is going.) This woman lived by herself in this huge house and hoarded cats. Nobody knows exactly how many lived there, but it was rumored to have been in the hundreds. She had been dead for many years by the time we looked at the property with her son, but the smell of cat urine throughout the building was distinct and ever present. The son had turned the building into apartments, but I use that term loosely. It was more of a flophouse. One unit that had been rented to a dancer who worked in the French Quarter had four inches of black sludge in the bathtub. Apparently she was too stoned to complain about it.

Another time, as I was giving a tour of the property to a prospective banker, with all of us in our business suits, the resident ferret from one of the units jumped up on my leg and started performing ferret sex. This was certainly not the typical PowerPoint presentation that banker was used to seeing!

And then there was Geno—a fixture in the neighborhood and at the neighborhood bars. He always wore a sailor hat, pulled an oxygen tank with one hand, and usually had a cigarette in the other. The irony of cause and effect was lost on him, but not on anyone else. Geno was probably in his sixties but looked a lot older. He lived in an add-on building in the back and was responsible for collecting the rent and generally keeping the ne'er-do-wells who lived there in order. In exchange, he lived for free.

Neal got the financing done again, and we bought the property for $600,000. Due to a combination of optimism, ignorance, and what the bank was willing to lend us, we borrowed an additional $300,000 for the renovations. This proved to be a colossal undercapitalization. But we were excited to take it on—oddball tenants, wacky property manager, cat piss, and all.

The experience of the renovation was a comedy in and of itself. We let the tenants stay while we got the renovation plans and pre-work done. One of them was a singing waiter in an Italian restaurant who on one occasion quite persistently asked that I take a charcoal drawing of Frank Sinatra instead of his $700 rent. "It was worth three times that amount," and he couldn't believe he was willing to part with it! Geno intervened and eventually collected the rent. In cash. That same day Geno asked me to lend him twenty dollars until his Social Security check came in ten days later. I figured this was the best investment I could ever make; the old man certainly wouldn't pay me back, and I could use that as a reason to never lend money to him again. Damned if he didn't pay me back exactly as promised, and I soon became Geno's banker.

Many homes on St. Charles Avenue—and across the city—had second-floor galleries used by the early residents to get some relief from the heat. During the 1960s, with the advent of air-conditioning, it became popular to enclose the galleries with glass and create an extra air-conditioned room. That was the case at 4228 St. Charles Avenue, and it was an eyesore. We ripped it out and set out to restore it to an open-air gallery. You would think everyone would be happy with this improvement, right? But instead, the Historic District Landmarks Commission insisted that we rebuild the structure exactly as it had been in 1892, and that we specifically custom lathe the balcony spindles to be replicas of the originals! They were not impressed with the generic railing spindles we purchased for the building, apparently. I went up and down St. Charles Avenue for blocks in each direction photographing every second-floor gallery.

I created what I thought was a compelling slideshow for the HDLC, documenting the fact that no two buildings had the same spindle, thus proving there was no community design being violated. Further and more important, I thought, was that the current fire code required the railings to be forty-two inches high. The spindles the HDLC wanted us to create would match the original thirty-eight-inch height. The State Fire Marshal holds the ultimate decision to grant a Certificate of Occupancy, so we *had* to make the railing forty-two inches in order to be able to open. They quietly heard me out, and then without discussion told me we had to do it their way. (And the worst part was—unlike the rest of city hall—the HDLC people wouldn't take supplements to grease the skids!)

A LITTLE COMMON SENSE, PLEASE

Now, in a beautiful city like New Orleans, we need oversight to ensure that the whole place doesn't end up looking like a bad suburb. But still, a little common sense to support people who are spending a ton of money to restore a dilapidated building would have been nice. This type of process repeats itself over and over—I recently saw where a developer had to restore the only standing wall of a building that had otherwise fallen down. The expense of doing this type of repair, as compared to the cost of putting up a new wall, is what scares people away.

We proceeded with our plans anyway, and one afternoon a group from the HDLC showed up with big yellow STOP WORK stickers and pasted them all over the front of the building. That might have daunted some people, but we knew the HDLC folks wouldn't be working on weekends and that they only had oversight over the exterior of the building. They couldn't stop us from doing anything on the inside. So we rounded up a crew, finished all of the exterior work including the gallery over a Saturday and Sunday, took down the yellow signs, and moved on. You always have to make every effort to do things the right way, but sometimes you just have to get creative.

The HDLC people came back a week or so later and wanted to know what happened to their signs and how the gallery got completed in spite of their order. I told them I didn't know anything about it. Eventually they moved on to harassing other enterprising civilians.

• • •

We were set to open the Avenue Inn for Mardi Gras 2001—about a year behind schedule and a million dollars over budget. Our banker had kept advancing us money to keep construction going in order to avoid getting stuck with a half-finished project. Neal had been overseeing most of the construction, so he took some time off and headed for Disney World with his family for Mardi Gras, leaving me to oversee the grand opening.

When you are opening a hotel, the best way to get the construction done by a certain date is to sell all the rooms. Contractors are inclined to drag the process out, as eventually more things will get added on to keep their cash spigot flowing. We were going down to the wire the Friday before Mardi Gras when everyone was checking in. The first group of guests showed up at 9:00 a.m. I told them the room was not ready and check-in was at 3:00 p.m. They insisted on seeing the room they were going to be assigned, and eventually I relented. It was going to be one of the nicest rooms we had, but at the time I showed it to them, the painter was still finishing things up, and the furniture was not yet in the room. They started to raise a stink about the construction, but all I could say at that point was "Check-in is at three, and there *will* be a room here by then!" They turned, left, and I never saw them again.

But once the painting was done and the furniture was in, things went pretty well over the weekend. Mardi Gras parades passed right in front of the property and everyone was enjoying themselves. On the morning of Fat Tuesday,[5] one of the guests on the first floor reported sewage backing up into her bathtub. I called the contractor, but there was no way he could

5   Mardi Gras Day—or "Fat Tuesday" in New Orleans—has to be put into context here. It is the one day of the year that everyone stops what they are doing and has a celebration. Far more people celebrate Mardi Gras than Christmas. My first Mardi Gras at the Sheraton, I naively went to work, as hotel people worked nights, weekends, and holidays. Outside of a skeleton crew at the front desk, you could have shot a cannon through the place and not hit an employee. That was an eye-opener into the New Orleans culture for me. (And by 10:00 a.m. I was doing tequila shots in the basement of the old Supreme Court building surrounded by graphics of fish kills being monitored by the Department of Wildlife and Fisheries. But that is another story . . .) Added to the universal shutdown is the fact that parades run through the city from dawn to dusk, so it is nearly impossible to get anywhere.

get Uptown on Mardi Gras Day. Then I went through the phone book and called every 24/7 plumber who advertised, but to no avail. One guy actually answered the phone, and when I told him what I needed, he said he had answered the phone by mistake and wasn't working that day. Desperate, I climbed under the building, looking for a big ON/OFF switch or something that might be obvious to this non-handyman. I did find a valve that, when turned, began releasing sewage from the pipe and spilling it all over the ground. Turned out that did the trick, and everything drained from then on—right out of their toilets and bathtubs and onto the ground under the building. I just shook my head and went for an early-morning beer. What could I do? The plumbers would be back to work tomorrow.

• • •

Around the time we were rebuilding the property on St. Charles Avenue, Neal got a call from a couple of men in Bunkie, Louisiana. They wanted to renovate and reopen a historic Main Street hotel that had been shuttered for many years, but they had been unsuccessful in getting financing for the project. Neal took one look at their business plan and informed them that they clearly didn't know anything about running a hotel—which was the first time they realized they had a problem. He connected us, and I wrote up a real business plan, got them financing, and signed on to oversee the construction and ultimately the management of the hotel once it opened. I set up a management company and began a regular commute to Bunkie.

Bunkie is in the central part of Louisiana, thirty miles south of Alexandria. When one of the owners was asked where Bunkie is, he replied, "Right on the border of Coon Ass and Redneck." If you know anything about rural Louisiana, that makes perfect sense: the transition from south to north, Catholic to Baptist, freewheeling to Bible Belt. Bunkie has a small yet charming Main Street with antique stores, lunch counters, and the typical trappings of a small town. From a hotel perspective, its best redeeming quality was that it was fifteen miles from a brand-new casino resort, and it wouldn't take much overflow to fill thirty-three rooms per night.

What it didn't have was any kind of a decent restaurant. At first, I stayed in a local motel that had a sports bar and restaurant attached to it, where I got insanely sick the first few times I had dinner. After that, I started staying up in Alexandria, which has an Applebee's and some other chain restaurants. (Living in New Orleans, you can hardly call that eating.) Eventually, I started making the six-hour round trip on a daily basis just so I could get something decent to eat at night. I was on the road at 5:00 a.m. and, with luck, back by 7:00 p.m.

About a week before the Bailey Hotel was scheduled to open with all the rooms sold out (the O'Hara way), I arrived at 8:00 a.m. to find the building vacant. Eventually, I found the general contractor and asked him where all the construction workers were. With a completely straight face he said, "It's opening day of squirrel season." My jaw dropped, and I was uncharacteristically speechless for a matter of minutes. Who shoots squirrels, anyway? And even if they do, who needs a season? They are everywhere! And, what on earth does this have to do with all these people not being at work when I am trying to get this hotel open? I had hired a general manager who was from Alexandria, and I went to him with my anguish. He wasn't happy about it either but wasn't surprised and just gave me a shrug. "What can you do? It's squirrel season."

I share these stories because being an entrepreneur is not a glamorous job, especially when you are just starting out and doing most things yourself. Every time you see somebody getting an award or featured in a glowing article in a magazine, remember that at one point they were probably standing in sewage on Mardi Gras Day or contending with the opening of squirrel season.

CHAPTER FIVE

BUILDING THE BUSINESS: THE BEST FEELING IN THE WORLD

"If you don't build your dream, someone else will hire you to help them build theirs."

—DHIRUBHAI AMBANI

Many of the most exciting days of my life have been when I either started a new company myself or supported another entrepreneur in starting theirs. Those are moments of incredible optimism and opportunity—combined with excitement about the unknown that lies ahead. In those moments, anything can happen—you have a brilliant idea that you are acting upon, and the possibilities are endless. A lot of people get nervous about the unknown, and that fear holds a lot of them back. But to me, the unknown is what makes it all so exciting. It's the best feeling in the world.

In early 1998, Chateau Louisiane was fully up and running. Most of the work was done during the mornings and in the evenings, which left me plenty of time during the day to work on other ambitions. Upon locking in the Tulane account, I set up a new company—Crescent Hospitality—to handle the hotel and related services I was doing for Tulane. Not too long after that, I got a call from Terry Jackson, who was director of sales at the first start-up I had joined. We had become friendly during my short stint there, and he was calling with a proposition. "I'm tired of doing all of this work, with somebody else getting all of the money for it. We could do this ourselves."

Fresh off the agreement with Rob Hailey at Tulane, my response was,

"Good idea, I already had that idea, and I am already doing it." Terry had a couple of loyal clients he could bring along, so we set up shop. He worked from his house in the suburbs, and I worked from the B&B in the Garden District, where I was living at the time. It was a different world then, and I always have to laugh when people ask me how I got started in business. My first line is, "I know you will have a hard time believing this, but before the Internet . . ." There really was such a time. People would call hotels looking for rooms during busy times, and they had to do it one hotel at a time. Not like today, when you have a citywide search at your fingertips. Plus, the hotel inventory in New Orleans back then was only about a third of what it is now, so any halfway busy time would have everything sold out from the center of town all the way to the airport.

We nurtured relationships with hotels and contracted blocks of rooms during big conventions and special events. Then we would go to all of the other hotels and let them know that when they were sold out, they should have people call us since we would have rooms. We sold a couple hundred rooms for a half dozen or so events each year. With no overhead, we were living *large*. So large, in fact, that the funniest part now is that the services that are the core of our business today—transportation, group dinners, and evening events—we didn't bother with. We sent those requests to what are now our competitors.

Late in the nineties, as it became more common for people to book hotel rooms on the Internet, we leveraged our hotel relationships and began an online hotel reservation system called Jazznethotels.com. We contracted with a company in Sri Lanka to handle our database. They charged us nothing up front and a small percentage of sales—once again, no overhead. We got the hotel contracts and loaded them all up. We had operated a tour desk in one of the hotels for a while and understood that side of the business, so we started a sister site called Jazznettours.com where people could book activities like city tours and swamp outings.

Hotels back then were still stuck in the practice of giving dirt-cheap wholesale rates to tour operators. They did this partly to attract international business, where there would often be two or three layers of middlemen, each marking a room up before it got to the end user. Internet companies were new, and since people didn't know where else to put us, we fell into that category. Except there were no layers between us and the end user! So we would get rates that were eighty to a hundred dollars less than what the hotels were selling themselves, mark them up thirty to forty dollars a night, and still be fifty dollars less than what the hotels were offering the rooms for on their own websites! I figured this would only last a short period of time, and I told Terry we needed to be planning for the end of that joy ride soon. But it lasted for *years*! And the big chains were the last to catch on. Today, low-price guarantees are a staple of online booking, but it was amazing how long we ran circles around companies that were millions of times larger than us.

Everything was on the upswing as we approached the busy fall season of 2001. I had three B&Bs open, each one larger than the one before. The hotel reservation business was strong, and we were practically Internet pioneers.

• • •

Then one morning, when I hadn't quite mustered the energy to get up, I had the TV tuned to one of the 24-hour news channels. Breaking news interrupted the regular programming, saying that a plane had hit the World Trade Center. I knew that area of New York very well. From my late teens, whenever I was in New York City, I would make a trip to the Windows on the World restaurant in the World Trade Center for cocktails and the amazing views of Manhattan, the Statue of Liberty, and all of the surrounding area. I also had a fraternity brother who worked in 3 World Trade, whose office I had visited. So I knew exactly what I was looking at. The first footage showed a small hole in one of the towers, and it seemed like perhaps a small plane had veered off course and made impact. But there was no mistaking when the next plane came into view—a full jetliner coming in for a direct hit. It was clearly no accident, and like the rest of the country, I forgot about work and stayed glued to the television the rest of the day. As bad as it was, on that day it seemed like nothing more than a news event. No one could imagine what the effects were going to be.

Travel came to a standstill for months. Every reservation we had on the books at all three B&Bs canceled. Group business for Crescent Hospitality dried up overnight. We kept thinking it was temporary, but it went on and on. I found myself with $25,000 in monthly mortgages for the three B&Bs, plus the other overhead expenses. The hole got deep quickly, and by November we were behind on all the mortgage payments. The bankers kept calling about their payments, and I kept asking them, "Haven't you watched the news? Nobody is traveling. We have no business." Apparently all the bankers in New Orleans had picked an inopportune time to stop watching television.

Eventually, the Maison Esplanade became the sacrificial lamb. Around this time, I was reading Richard Branson's book *Losing My Virginity*. There is a passage in it where he comments that every successful entrepreneur has had to put a company into bankruptcy by the time he is thirty-five. And that is exactly what happened to Maison Esplanade, LLC. So I was thirty-four, and I had put a company into bankruptcy. I didn't take any consolation from Branson's words, but I did take some hope—he had certainly turned out just fine.

I played musical chairs with the finances of the other two B&Bs and Crescent Hospitality until we found a buyer for the Avenue Inn, which was finally all built out with nineteen rooms. It was a beautiful property on a wonderful stretch of St. Charles Avenue, and we had gone through so much work to get to that point. But the banker had now lent us a million dollars more than he had originally planned, and he was in as much trouble as we were over the deal—probably a lot more. I hated to see it go, but we did each pocket $20,000 of the $1.8 million selling price. Not much, for all the work and heartache, but it was better than a loss. It was time to pull up the bootstraps and move along.

• • •

While all of this was going on, we were busy looking for ways to grow Crescent Hospitality. Terry was not involved with the B&Bs, so he had been spared that anguish. He came across a company called PRA Destination Management that had franchise opportunities available. Buying a franchise would be an opportunity for us to broaden our client base and take advantage of the systems and infrastructure that PRA had developed. We had stopped sending additional services to our competitors a few years earlier because we had sensed the market was tightening up— so this was a perfect fit for us.

The franchise team was welcoming, and we could tell that their philosophy on customer service and team loyalty aligned with ours. They were impressed with how ingrained we were in the hotel community and excited about the prospects the two guys from the Big Easy brought to the table. We purchased the franchise for Louisiana and the Mississippi Gulf Coast in 2002, establishing PRA Destination Management New Orleans.

DESTINATION MANAGEMENT COMPANIES

Destination Management Companies (DMCs) are the creative and logistics experts behind travel-based business events. Everybody knows what hotel they stayed in and who the keynote speaker was, but few people realize that there is an entire industry managing the rest of the experience. And frankly, if we do a good job, you likely won't ever know we are here! The evening events in spectacular local venues? Your DMC. Your group dinners at the best local restaurants? Your DMC. The tours and excursions that are provided to your group, the decor and entertainment in the hotel ballroom, and even the transportation from the airport and to your events were most likely designed and executed by your local DMC.

Things started slowly, as they always do. Every time you start a new company you are excited for the prospects and are confident that you have such a good idea and plan that it will take off right out of the gate. That is the nature of starting new businesses. After all, if you didn't think so, you wouldn't start the business in the first place! We were optimistic that with our contacts and the backing of PRA, we would steamroll our way to success. As is often the case, the entrenched competition did not want the newcomers treading on their soil. A lesson to new entrepreneurs: *Never* underestimate the competition, and resist the temptation to overestimate the size of the market. The competition quickly circled the wagons on their hotel relationships. As long as we were mainly booking hotel rooms, we all got along and they let us do our thing. But hotels are a very good source of referrals for DMCs, and now that we were a full-on DMC, all bets were off.

No matter what business you are in, it is hard to land the big, lucrative clients until you have a track record, and you can't build a track record until you have some big, lucrative clients. It's a vicious cycle that drives many new entrepreneurs to despair. But every time we got turned down, Terry just said, "That just means we are that much closer to the next win." We took the small things that came our way, kept overhead low, and remained optimistic and persistent. We had a small office downtown and we hired an account manager, but beyond that, our expenses were minimal. Our bank officer was understanding of the needs of a growing company and worked with us when our account hit red numbers.

It was just Terry, two employees, and I, but our business did grow, and at one point we made the heady decision to poach a sales manager from one of our competitors. She commanded a salary well in excess of anything we could realistically afford and more than we were paying ourselves. But we were banking on the belief that she would bring a book of clients and hotel relationships with her, and that the resulting new business would easily cover the investment. It took us about a year to reach the unfortunate conclusion that things were not working for anyone, and we parted ways, much poorer for the experiment. I have heard Norm Brodsky speak several times at conferences, and one of the things he preaches is that there are no shortcuts in growing a business; it is best to do it organically. Resisting the temptation to hire a competitor's sales person is one of the things he always talks about. I always think about this episode when I hear him and think *how right you are, Norm!* It turns out that most people who are willing to jump to a competitor bring more baggage than benefit.

All of this took place between 1997 and 2005, and eight years into the entrepreneurial journey I had experienced some setbacks, had some successes, and learned a lot of lessons. But damn, I was having fun!

CHAPTER SIX

THE SAINTS ARE COMING: 2006–2008

"Success is how high you bounce when you hit bottom."

—GENERAL GEORGE PATTON

As the end of August 2005 rolled around and we were enjoying our weekend in Pensacola, we didn't know there was any reason to be anything other than optimistic. As we know now, the world was about to completely change for all of us.

In the months after Katrina, I bounced around the southeast United States. I spent time with my godparents in Hilton Head, with friends in Atlanta and Tallahassee, and had free rein of a place on the beach in Seaside, Florida, courtesy of a friend I made on the board of directors of the Society of Hosts, which is the alumni association of the hospitality school at Florida State.

About a week after I left New Orleans, I was playing golf with my godfather at his course in South Carolina. When we came back to the clubhouse, CNN was on the TV monitor with a live feed of a major fire in my neighborhood. News coverage of New Orleans was twenty-four hours a day, and it was all bad. It was at that point that I realized I couldn't watch the coverage any longer. It was heartbreaking and it just made me feel even worse. (It was also hard to avoid, as even during sporting events on TV, they would interrupt for breaking news updates.)

It was almost a month before the authorities would let anyone return to the city. Armed National Guard troops were stationed at every road coming into New Orleans to keep people out. In mid-September, I made a trip back to see what I could find out. At the time, anyone who was trying to reopen a restaurant was given a special permit to enter the city because restaurants were needed to feed the emergency crews working in the city. I got hold of one of these permits from Vic and made my way into the city as a purported Fat Harry's employee to get my first look at the damage.

I certainly expected the worst, so nothing was going to come as a surprise. During the time I had been hopscotching around, there was pretty much constant television coverage of flooding and looting and fires—and madness. The Superdome is home to the New Orleans Saints and is a centerpiece of the skyline of downtown New Orleans. When the waters rose, the Dome was opened as a shelter of last resort for people fleeing their inundated homes, and it quickly became overwhelmed by the number of people sheltered there and a focus of the news coverage of the tragedies playing out. Even the area around it was surrounded by water, so when buses came in from out of state to evacuate people, they couldn't get near the building. There were stories of suicides, murders, and rapes in the degenerating and squalid conditions inside the building. And while the official city position does not substantiate any of those stories, it doesn't seem like much of a stretch to believe them.

So when I made my foray back in, I had no doubt that it was going to be a mess—which it was. The crew at Fat Harry's was working to clean out coolers, scrub everything down, and try to get in a position to open. There was a lot of money to be made if they could, and they were one of the first to do so.

I grabbed a couple of the guys and went over to my house. We dragged all of the furniture and appliances out to the street, where city dump trucks would periodically come through and pick everything up that had been piled at the curb. You had to get all these things out of the house as quickly as possible, because they were wet and full of mold already. The tenants who rent the other side of my double had texted me that they had credit cards and a bunch of cash in the freezer and asked if I would retrieve it for them. Naively, Bradley and I opened the freezer door and were immediately overwhelmed by the stench of food that had been rotting in the heat and the dark for three weeks. That—plus the smell and sight of the maggots that were feasting on the food—was sickening, and we both had to work to keep from throwing up on the spot. We duct-taped the refrigerator doors closed so they wouldn't open as we dragged it out to the curb. The money and credit cards are still there—wherever that fridge ended up.

I went to check out our office, which was on the fourth floor of a five-story building downtown. The first floor had flooded, but outside of a couple of broken windows, we didn't have any damage there. After the city began allowing people back in, the landlord started calling me to ask whether we were going to move back in. I knew it would be a while before we had any business, and I didn't want to have to pay rent, so I kept putting him off.

I thought that would be easy enough to do, but there were some criminal defense lawyers on the first floor whose office had flooded, and they suddenly had a lot of new work defending the looters who were locked up around the state. They were ready to pay rent and offered to move up to our floor. The landlord gave me the option to start paying rent right away or lose the space to the lawyers. Terry came down and picked up all of our furniture and computers, and they spent the next couple of years in his garage in Slidell.

THE AMERICAN PEOPLE

Of all the destruction, heartache, and frustration that resulted from the spectacular failure of the levees, the thing that sticks with me the most is the goodness of heart of the American people. Close friends and total strangers alike provided offers of help and support to me. I had job offers all over the place and couldn't pay for a drink anywhere. Heck—a complete stranger in a bar in Seaside went back to his condo to get a book he thought I would like. An old friend from college stuck a couple of hundred bucks in my pocket, and when I protested that I didn't need the money, he said, "Maybe not now, but you might later." In

continued

the uncertainty, he had a point. All of this was unsolicited. The instances of offers and actual help are far too numerous to recount, but I want to make it loud and clear that in spite of all of the distracting bickering that dominates the news cycles, on the street, the American people are good people, reflecting the spirit of the early settlers and our Founding Fathers. We will find a way to get it done, and we will help our fellow man. For years, school groups, church groups, and business groups came to New Orleans by the thousands to build houses with Habitat for Humanity and rebuild schools with the Recovery School District.

After a couple of months, it was time for me to find either a temporary or a permanent home. Heather had moved back into her second-floor condo on the fringe of the suburbs, and in spite of losing her job in the hospitality industry (who didn't!), she was intent on sticking it out and making it work.

Nowhere to Go and No One to Answer To

For me, the state of the city was such a depressing mess that I couldn't bear to look at it every day. I was staying at Heather's when I was in town and hitting the gym during the day after answering what few business-related emails I received. By mid-afternoon I was at Fat Harry's—which was quite the scene. It was flat-out *packed* by four o'clock every afternoon. And there was not a woman to be found anywhere. Families had relocated out of town so the children could go to school, and the men were in New Orleans rebuilding their homes and their businesses. Add to that the relief workers that were here, and nobody had anywhere to go or anyone to answer to when the day ended.

The drive from Fat Harry's to Heather's condo at the end of the day was surreal. The power was still out throughout most of the city, so there were no stoplights and no traffic enforcement. Once the sun went down, it was pitch dark. You just drove as fast as you wanted and stopped when you thought you needed to. Then, as the parish line approached, you'd see the lights of Jefferson Parish lighting up the sky. The last thing I passed each night before crossing the line was a colossal debris field that had been set up in a park outside of the Lakeview neighborhood, which had taken a direct hit from the failure of the 17th Street Canal. All day long, there was a steady stream of dump trucks hauling debris out of the debris field to landfills, and just as quickly, dump trucks bringing in more debris from the neighborhood. It was a mile long and ten blocks wide, and it never got smaller. It was just a massive pile of people's life possessions.

Clearly, our business was not coming back any time soon, if at all. Every day, we learned about another group or convention that had to pull out of the city, and the dates they were pulling out from were further and further in the future. I needed a change of scenery as much as I needed something to do. I had a couple of job offers in Tallahassee and a lot of friends there, but it didn't seem like the fresh start I needed. I discussed the options with Heather. She was not happy about it but agreed to try to make things work long distance.

. . .

Ski season was approaching, so I called a friend, Tom McNeill, who owns a catering company in Vail, Colorado. I told him I was trying to figure out what to do and was thinking about coming out to Vail. Tom's response? "Well, come on out. You can live with me and you can work for me." Considering those were two of the most important things I was lacking at the moment—a place to live and a job—I told him I would start packing and be on my way. (Packing didn't take long. All I had with me was the original duffel bag I'd brought when I left my house.)

So off I went to Vail, the beneficiary of the generosity of Tom McNeill. Tom used to be a chef at the Sheraton New Orleans. He moved to Vail to work at a hotel there and ended up opening a popular catering company

called Gourmet Cowboy. I did catering work for Tom and contract operations work for a local Destination Management Company. Then I got a job
on the mountain setting up ski races to gain a season ski pass.

But the biggest break I received was when PRA called and offered jobs
to Terry and me, working for the PRA global sales team while our office
was closed. This was crucial in allowing us to maintain the contacts and
client relationships that would help us kick-start things when the office
opened back up. My partner took on a full-time role and I agreed to a half-
time role. I was stressed and antsy and didn't want to commit to sitting
at a desk forty hours a week. So I worked twenty hours a week for PRA
from Vail and split the rest of the time between the other three jobs. It all
worked out, and I got lots of skiing in.

PRA originally was called Patti Roscoe and Associates, and rebranded
to PRA Destination Management as the company expanded. Our legendary founder, Patti Roscoe, decided to go out on her own in 1981 and open
a Destination Management Company. Things were radically different
then, and she was told many times, in no uncertain terms, that this was
no role for a woman. But Patti had some clients who believed in her, and
she built a team and a company around world-class customer service and
taking care of each other. I imagine in those early days the latter was especially important because the outside was full of disbelievers. She was no
patsy in the business world, but she had the ability to inspire and motivate
the team by having a genuine personal bond.

That two people have more than thirty years with PRA, and a half
dozen more are approaching or past twenty years is a testament to the
success you can have when you take care of your team. This is not a business that makes anyone great fortunes, so you have to do it with intangibles. Patti reinforced a belief I always have held and that isn't reflected in
the corporate world often enough. She is a role model and mentor to me,
and the time I get to spend with her is as rewarding as anything I do. The
turnover at AlliedPRA New Orleans has always been minimal, and it is the
belief in taking care of your team and creating the intangible motivators
that keep them believing in me and the company.

So it should come as no surprise that Patti wasn't going to let her two "New Orleans boys" go this alone. Even though there was no real need to add to the global sales team at the time (and frankly, we probably didn't pull our proper weight), that was secondary to our well-being in the eyes of Patti and the leadership at PRA. Many of our competitors did not reemerge after Katrina, and many others were in start-up mode after shutting down for two years. But once business was ready to come back to New Orleans, we were able to hit the ground running—because we had been working the market, attending trade shows, and making client calls throughout. We had a head start on the competition as a result of the foresight and compassion of Patti and her team.

· · ·

While I had established a base of operations in Vail and pieced tougher enough part-time work to sustain myself, there was also the issue of the flooded-out house back in New Orleans. Although my house had only taken on about six inches of water, the water sat there for two weeks in the stifling heat before receding. By the time I got back in September, the entire interior and everything I owned was covered with mold. Water was also coming in through the roof where the shingles had blown off, and so every time it rained, more water soaked the upper floors. The house would have to be totally gutted and rebuilt.

Enter Shane Porter. He owns a business that builds and repairs furniture, specializing in antiques. He is the best in the business by far, and all of the Uptown blue bloods go to him for their needs. During Katrina, his shop took on eight feet of water, and much of the custom-made equipment he used for his work was destroyed. Like a lot of people, he needed work, and like many, he had to find it outside of his normal career. He had done construction and home renovations when he was younger and had a friend with a contractor's license, so they went to work renovating houses.

It was a small operation, just Shane and a young man from Honduras named Jeffrey, ironically enough. Shane did all of the woodwork, Jeffrey did the grunt work, and they subbed out the plumbing, electricity, et cetera. This was a godsend for me. Shane and I had been friends for as long as I have lived in New Orleans. While many people struggled to find contractors, or got stiffed by unscrupulous ones, I was able to give Shane the keys to the kingdom and let him run with them. I fully trusted all the decisions he made and never questioned his expenses. He was doing it so cost-effectively that on numerous occasions I had to ask if he was paying himself anything. He assured me he was being fairly compensated. To this day, I don't know how much he paid himself, but it was all based on trust, and I got one of the best renovation experiences of anyone I know.

Prior to Katrina, we didn't have many people from Mexico or Central America in New Orleans. There wasn't any obvious reason for this; it just seemed like the immigration path stopped before it got to Lake Charles, on the western border with Texas. Purely speculating here, but southwest Louisiana is predominantly Cajun, and the Cajuns are not afraid of hard work either, so maybe there just weren't jobs to attract new immigrants. That all changed after Katrina. There was lots of work, and it was *hard*, dirty work. People would come in from Atlanta or Dallas or wherever and leave in a day. Meanwhile, the immigrant workers were making significantly more than they could make back home. Jeffrey, like many of them, sent his earnings back home to his extended family. One man told me he sent all of his construction earnings home to Mexico to put his brother through medical school. He was so clearly proud as he told me this. It is no exaggeration to say that the city of New Orleans was rebuilt on the backs of our friends from south of the border. Many have stayed and have been a great addition to our community.

THE BACKS OF OUR FRIENDS

The immigration system in this country is so out of whack it is ridiculous. It has become such an emotional issue that there is no chance for true problem solving. Everyone is either "let 'em all in" or "throw 'em all out."

The fact of the matter is that we need people of many different skill levels to keep our economy humming. Do you think you could buy a head of lettuce if we threw 'em all out? Likewise, many people come from other countries to study engineering and science in the best universities in the United States. Then they can't get a job here because of their immigration status, and they take their talents elsewhere. Meanwhile Apple, Google, and Facebook are screaming for more engineers and can't get the talent they need domestically. What we need is to drop the rhetoric on immigration and find solutions that let hardworking, law-abiding people live here and fill the jobs that we need filled.

Thankfully, I had Shane to handle my house renovation, but there were many other things that got in the way of progress for me and for others. Many people struggled with their insurance companies, waiting well into the new year for insurance settlements. I caught a break here as well: My father knew a lawyer in New York who specialized in insurance settlements. He did the work with the insurance company and took a cut of the proceeds, while I ended up with a better net settlement, much faster than I ever could have received on my own. This guy was a bulldog and quite entertaining to boot—provided he was on your side. But that is when things came to a grinding halt. The insurance company settled in a matter of weeks and sent the proceeds to the mortgage company to escrow. The mortgage company claimed they were so backed up they could not process the release of funds to me, which I needed to begin renovations. This repeated every time a new round of funding was sent by the insurance company. I spent well over a hundred hours on the phone, sent dozens of faxes to various departments, and got consistently stonewalled. The reality of it is, when the bank is sitting on tens of millions of dollars in insurance proceeds, every extra day they can hold it makes them money on the float—pretty cruel to people who are trying to get their lives back together.

The stress that people were going through at this time could only be fathomed if you were here. It cracked marriages and relationships, and caused a lot of pain and suffering, literally and figuratively. One friend of mine committed suicide over the stress of rebuilding and his resulting failing marriage. Another broke his arm cleaning up his yard and developed a staph infection under his cast. By the time he realized it, the infection had spread, and it killed him. There was serious trauma going on, and we all felt it firsthand.

That time I cried for the first time in thirty years on the highway in Mississippi? It happens all the time now. If I read about Katrina, or just see a sad or happy story in general, it happens. I read recently that this could be linked to a symptom of PTSD. Maybe it is, maybe it isn't, but it had never happened before this.

It Was Those Kinds of Times, and Everyone Had a Story

After a year in Vail, I moved back to New Orleans. I had considered staying longer in Colorado, and even staying permanently. But on my visits back to the city, I could feel the vibe coming back, and as people were getting more settled, the bonds between old friends became stronger than ever from coming through so much shared adversity together. "How much water did you get?" became a standard starting point when seeing someone you had not seen in a long time. I remember one friend saying, "Only about six inches." People sighed with relief until she added, "On the second floor . . ." It was those kinds of times, and everyone had a story.

In the first years after Katrina, coming back to New Orleans was hard. Nothing was normal, and the easy route would be to do something else. But this created a great spirit among the people who were here fighting it out, because you really had to want to be here. You know the analogy of the ham-and-egg breakfast and the difference between being involved and being committed: The chicken is involved; the pig is committed. Well, the people who were here rebuilding their lives and businesses were *committed*!

I was still working twenty hours a week for PRA, as there was still no movement by way of groups coming back to the city. Vic LaBorde had left Fat Harry's and opened a bar and grill in the suburbs called Tarpon Joe's—an ode to the many years a group of us spent fishing in Islamorada in the Florida Keys. At night I made the trek to the burbs and managed the place for him.

September 25, 2006, was a bellwether day in the rebuilding of New Orleans. The bond the city shares with the New Orleans Saints—in spite of forty years of futility up until then—is unparalleled in professional sports in the United States. In 2005 the Saints played one home game in New York and the rest in Baton Rouge and San Antonio. Saints owner Tom Benson was keenly interested in using Katrina as an excuse to move the team to San Antonio, but NFL Commissioner Paul Tagliabue put the stop to that and insisted that the league would not turn its back on New Orleans. With some incentive from the NFL, Doug Thornton and his team at SMG worked around the clock for a year to get the stadium ready to host NFL football. During the aftermath of Katrina, the Dome was an international symbol of the despair and chaos of the storm, the low socioeconomic status of those who sheltered there, and a source of the terrible scenes that were blasted around the world for years.

But miraculously, Doug and his team had the iconic stadium ready for NFL football on that Monday night. ESPN was featuring the matchup between the Saints and archrival Atlanta Falcons, which drew a then-record fifteen million viewers. Fans gathered for hours in advance of the doors opening to celebrate the homecoming and to greet friends they hadn't seen in over a year. The pregame activities served to heighten the enthusiasm, capped when U2 and Green Day joined forces in an amazing rendition of the Skids' song "The Saints Are Coming," just prior to kickoff. That song has been an anthem for the city ever since. Anybody who lived through Katrina stops and sings when it comes on. By kickoff, the crowd was about to burst with emotion.

Atlanta received the kickoff and was stopped on three downs and forced to punt. On the punt, an undersized special teams ace named Steve

Gleason came clean through the line and blocked the punt, which was then recovered in the end zone by Curtis Deloatch for a touchdown. The announcers, coaches, players, and fans will all tell you they have never heard anything as loud as the explosion of euphoria at that moment as a year's worth of pent-up emotions came pouring out of the New Orleans fans. The Saints went on to pummel the Falcons 23–3, and at that point everybody knew that in spite of what was still in front of them, everything was going to be all right. A statue of Steve Gleason in midair as he blocked that punt now stands on the concourse outside the Superdome.

Sadly, in 2011 Steve revealed that he had been diagnosed with ALS, commonly known as Lou Gehrig's disease. There is no cure and it is a cruel killer as it attacks the nerve cells in the brain and spinal cord. He has bravely fought this publicly and has already outlived his expectancy at diagnosis. He has been the face of people suffering with the disease in many ways, lobbying Congress for research and support funding and raising research funds through his Team Gleason foundation, whose motto is *No White Flags*. Having lost his ability to speak, he communicates through a specialized computer that he controls with his eye movements. Research that he has prompted has led to a number of innovations to benefit the way people with ALS live with the disease.

One and the Same

2006 also saw the arrival of Sean Payton as head coach and Drew Brees as quarterback of the Saints. The once-hapless Saints suddenly became a contender in the NFL, reaching the playoffs that first season and then in 2009 making a heart-stopping run all the way to Super Bowl Champions. The Saints' growing success paralleled the recovery of the city, and most people consider it one and the same. When Garrett Hartley kicked the game-winning field goal to win the NFC Championship, I was in the upper terrace of the Superdome with a group of longtime friends, and all these grown men cried and hugged and carried on like nobody's business. Emotional still, four and a half years later.

When Tracy Porter intercepted Peyton Manning and raced for the game-clinching touchdown in the Super Bowl, he was running straight toward the seats where Vivian and I were sitting in Hard Rock Stadium in Miami. I turned to her in complete disbelief and screamed, "You know we just won the f***king Super Bowl!!!" And then the tears poured out. Of course they did . . .

It was a statement of how far we had come in such unlikely circumstances, a city and a team that so many people had given up on.

• • •

In late 2006, we had started to get some interest in the city. Terry and I set up shop in the dining room of my house and set about letting everybody know we were back in business. This started with the local hotel community, which was certainly unsure about who had made it through and who had not. Lots of happy reunions took place here. Industry events were still a bit of a somber experience, dominated by talk about who ended up in which far-flung locale. Nobody had business, so there was nothing to discuss there.

But slowly, bits and pieces started coming in, and once again the PRA relationship was golden. Even though we were locally owned, there was clearly a feeling in the client community that the strong brand of PRA would protect against any financial issues. We started getting calls from clients we had never heard from before. Stories of clients losing deposits as our competitors went out of business had made their way through the meeting-planner community, so they were hesitant to send deposits to New Orleans. Our brand gave them confidence in us, so clients who had other relationships in the city prior to Katrina were now coming to us. At one point I came home to find a check for a quarter of a million dollars in the mailbox. Things were starting to roll!

Things picked up faster for us than what I heard from our competitors, but I was still nervous about the uncertainty. We kept working out of my dining room for long after it turned out to be necessary, but after all I had been through financially and emotionally I was hesitant to take on overhead. Even when making progress, you were always expecting the other shoe to drop. We hired an operations manager on a contract basis just to work the events, and she joined us in the dining room on days when she was working. To this day I make extensive use of contract staff, even in management positions, to minimize overhead. There are highly qualified people out there who like the flexibility of contract work and don't want to come to an office. It is something every fast-growing company should consider.

So here we were, ten years into the history of the company, and we were essentially a start-up again. We had to develop a brand-new go-to-market strategy, but in this case with one *huge* albatross around our neck. While the meeting-planner community was generally supportive of doing business in New Orleans and helping the city get back on its feet, all it took was one executive in an organization with concerns to squash an opportunity. We had to go out and tell our story in the face of an unending barrage of negative publicity. I remember sitting in clients' offices in 2010—*five years later*—and people asking me if the city was still underwater. This was a common occurrence. You could deem them ignorant, but CNN was running pictures of the flooded city for years, so those images were embedded in people's brains long after the city had returned to normal operation. It was a very frustrating time, and to this day when somebody speaks poorly of New Orleans I take it as a personal affront.

Here we were, though, hitting the road to tell the world that New Orleans was open for business. We traveled to key client markets and made countless presentations, banded together to host receptions at industry trade shows, and brought groups of prospective clients to the city on familiarization tours. It cost a lot of money that nobody had, but we were in survival mode and knew that we needed to generate momentum if we were to succeed. Everybody in the hospitality industry was doing it. It was a united effort and one of the multitude of things that bonded the community after Katrina. When you are contending with so much rejection, there is comfort in kindred souls. Like Billy Joel famously said, "It's better than drinking alone."

CHAPTER SEVEN

THE REBUILD: FISHING WHERE THE FISH ARE

"The difference between a successful person and others is not a lack of strength, not a lack of knowledge, but rather a lack of will."

—VINCE LOMBARDI

I am a firm believer in fishing where the fish are. You have to be out in front of your potential customers, meeting them face-to-face. You can meet them at trade shows or at their office, or somewhere in their city—but the only way to build a lasting relationship is to see them, be with them. You simply cannot create large-scale B-to-B sales over the Internet. Often, companies facing difficult financial times cut back on travel, as they somehow view it as a discretionary expense. The reality is quite the opposite. When you don't take the time to visit your customers, you'll soon have fewer sales, and less money to spend on sales activities, and on it goes in a downward spiral. So, even though we had very little available cash, I was on the road visiting potential customers.

As I mentioned earlier, this was a daunting process. Some people took our appointments just so they could hear stories about the flood, even though they had no desire to do any business in the city. Some people said they would love to bring groups to New Orleans, but said, "We have execs who don't think the city is ready." And every once in a while, the stars would line up, and someone would want to hear our story *and* had interest in bringing a group or two to the city.

Throughout all of this, our partnership with PRA was a priceless asset. Sales trips coordinated by global sales managers included multiple PRA offices, so we were able to gain meetings with people who might have stuck with their false perception of New Orleans. But they met with us because of the other destinations that were part of the presentations. Once I was in the door, I worked to counter their misperceptions and was able to convert enough of them into believers to get us going. It was no easy task and having thick skin and persistence was mandatory. The good news is, all successful salespeople have thick skin and persistence in abundance.

At the same time, we had to build the operational side of the enterprise. Many of our suppliers had gone out of business, and many more reopened but without the same quality they possessed before the flood. Sometimes it was their physical property and sometimes it was their staff who was not up to their previous quality. As a DMC, our clients rely on us to be the experts in our destination and to have our ears to the ground. Venues may have pretty pictures on the Internet, but they are not always that way in person. Sometimes a couple of blocks off the main thoroughfare in any city can make for a dangerous location, but you might not guess it from looking at a map.[6] And certainly restaurant reviews from 2004 or 2005 were no longer applicable in 2007. So not only was *our* business like a start-up in 2007—the entire industry was!

We set out to renew relationships with the people we had worked with before, many of whom were in new jobs and new places. We had to vet the quality of anything and everything we were going to propose to incoming groups. Clients were particularly sensitive to quality issues, and rightfully so. A lot had changed.

---

6   This is true every day in the business-events world, not just after a disaster. One of the primary values we bring to a client is the up-to-the-minute knowledge of what is taking place in our destination. That means knowing how road construction or special events (parades are almost a daily occurrence in New Orleans!) will impact a transportation move. That means knowing which restaurants are up and coming and, conversely, which ones are on the downslope. It means knowing which venues are appropriate for certain types of events and which are not. For example, in a historic city like New Orleans, there are some amazing historic venues, but if you want to do an awards dinner, you have to know which ones have sight lines to the stage. There are lots of load-bearing columns in old buildings. DMCs have to understand their clients' objectives and select restaurants, venues, and events that advance the clients' goals.

Restaurants that were great before Katrina were slow to get back up to speed, and many event venues still had websites up—but the establishments were, in fact, closed. Most tour companies were very slow to come back up to their previous standards simply because there wasn't much business for tours. (Well, except the one tour people couldn't get enough of—the one that went through the Ninth Ward and other areas that were hardest hit; the city council finally passed an ordinance prohibiting tours through these areas, as residents complained that they felt like animals in a zoo as tour buses full of people gawked at them.) So you really had to be on the ground knowing what was going on.

We still owed some suppliers money from before the storm, but despite using the income from all my side jobs, there wasn't enough to take care of everyone right away. I spoke with the owner of every business we owed money to and gave them realistic expectations of when they would get what they were owed. I gave my word that we would make them whole. In no instance did we even think about trying to negotiate down our debt. These were all small-business owners just like us, struggling to get by in a changed world. They were family-owned restaurants, local transportation companies, and small tour operators. They were already dealing with enough people who had gone out of business—or simply stiffed them. I gave them my word that they would be paid, and we were able to resume doing business on that basis. And every single company got paid on time or early.[7]

---

7   There was one hiccup in the process of making everyone whole, and it provides a valuable lesson in the types of people you'll meet along the way. Before Katrina hit, we processed a payment to the general manager of a motor coach company we did business with, but he hadn't deposited the check. About three weeks after Katrina, he called me to ask if he could deposit it. I asked him not to, since all of our company funds were being used to cover our living expenses. We were very short at the moment, and besides, I hadn't even been let back into the city to evaluate our office and my house. "Give me some time," I advised, "and I will make sure you get paid." Well, he deposited the check anyway, and when it was returned NSF, rather than work it out with me, he turned it over to the district attorney! So I was facing a criminal charge for writing bad checks. Fortunately, the DA was not only understanding of the situation, but she was rather incredulous that the guy had done what he did. I set up a payment plan, paid off the check and the not-insignificant DA's fees, and that was the end of the matter. He never got another dime from me. This guy is a world-class asshole. But in the end it is his loss—he used to be our primary motor coach provider, and in the years since then, we have spent millions of dollars with his competitors that would have otherwise gone to him. Just because he couldn't wait a little bit for a few thousand dollars.

As a result of that, our credit is good in the city to this day. People who used to call me when we owed them a few thousand dollars now routinely run $50,000 tabs for us. Of course, since we have grown so quickly, we can run up $50,000 tabs a lot faster than we did in the past!

CASH FLOW

PRA New Orleans had been growing rapidly by 2005, and we were playing the cash-in, cash-out game like all growing companies do. As long as we kept booking business and cash was coming in, it all worked. I remember an accounting professor I had at Tulane telling the class, "Never mind the P&L statement—the only statement to focus on when you are running a company is the cash-flow statement." I was living in the corporate world at the time, so I couldn't relate to what he was saying, but for some reason, it stuck in my mind. As it turns out, truer words were never spoken. In a simple example, if you are booking a lot of business, but the clients are not paying quickly, you can have a great-looking P&L statement but basically have no money. You can't pay the rent or make the payroll with paper profits. Likewise, you can lose money for years, but as long as you find a way to have cash flow, you can stay in business.

When Katrina hit, the spigot suddenly turned off for a lot of people. A number of my competitors got caught with their pants down and went out of business owing a lot of people money—including clients who had paid them deposits for future groups. Some of them were very established brands. We were hit hard, but I spoke with every company we owed money to—transportation companies, restaurants, decor suppliers, small businesses all—explained what the schedule was, and assured them that we would make them all whole, eventually. A lot of the money I used to pay off my debts came from working other jobs rather than taking revenue from the company, but I was showing good-faith efforts, and that was enough for everybody.

There are a million reasons why growing companies burn cash. Their clients may be slow to pay, they may hire in anticipation of new work that hasn't generated revenue yet, they may have invested in technology or other assets . . . the list goes on. It's always important to maintain good credit, so that when demands on your cash exceed the speed at which it's coming in, you are not suddenly in rough water with your suppliers.

Some companies make squeezing suppliers part of their business model. I don't ever do that. They have businesses to run as well, and if we ran such hard terms as to make them unprofitable, we wouldn't have them around to do business with.

SUPPLIER RELATIONSHIPS

It is often stated that a chain is only as good as its weakest link. But still, many companies treat their suppliers like second-class citizens. In our business, our contract staff and the employees of our suppliers—bus drivers, servers, event staff—are the ones on the front lines with our guests. They have to buy in to our service philosophy and understand our expectations in the same way our full-time staff does. You can't browbeat people into doing things your way in the service business. You have to make them feel like the important part of the team that they are. So we are constantly doing supplier outreach events to ensure they are on board.

Every August when it is the slow season in New Orleans, we do a supplier appreciation party. I am always thrilled at how many people turn up for this. We treat them to a night of food and drinks, and raffle off prizes like gift cards, bottles of wine, and other things that they can happily put to use. We get so many appreciative comments and letters about our party, and it is regularly pointed out that we are the only company like ours who does such an event.

During the year, we recognize our suppliers on social media, send thank-you notes when they handle a particularly intensive group, and

continued

keep them engaged with regular communications, office visits, and impromptu celebrations to ensure that we are top of mind with them. Doing these things ensures that they understand our message and who we are. Then when times are busy, we are a priority for their best service, people, and equipment.

Our competitors all have the opportunity to use the same suppliers that we do, and our clients know that. But when I am able to assure our clients that we get the best service from the best suppliers on their behalf, it is a differentiator for us.

In simplest terms, if you are a restaurant specializing in seafood, and there is an unexpected shortage of shrimp, wouldn't you want to be on the best terms with your shrimp supplier so that you are first in line?

No discussion of Katrina would be complete without a quick look at one C. Ray Nagin, who was the mayor of New Orleans at the time Katrina hit. He was especially notable in my world because of the numerous, widely covered rants he went on during the couple of years after the storm. As a result, I found myself constantly questioned by clients, friends, and complete strangers about his competency. He claimed he was going to make New Orleans a "chocolate city," said the murder rate in the city post-Katrina was a bad thing "but it keeps the New Orleans brand out there," and that God was sending hurricane after hurricane because He was mad at America over Iraq, among other things. When people questioned me about him, my explanation was that the man was under a terrible amount of stress given the circumstances, and that since nobody could put themselves in his shoes, they couldn't possibly understand his behavior. I even voted for him again in 2006. (Of course, he was running against Mitch Landrieu, so I would have voted for just about anyone else. Landrieu went on to become another terrible mayor from 2011 to 2018.)

Ray Nagin was the area general manager for Cox Communications when he ran for mayor in 2002. He ran as the classic outsider/businessman who was going to fix the corruption in city hall and run New Orleans like a business. He was in the Executive MBA class ahead of me at Tulane in 1994, so I knew who he was. I voted for him in 2002, knowing from my experiences at city hall that it definitely needed shaking up. As it turns out, he fell victim to the temptations of government largesse and was ultimately convicted on twenty of twenty-one charges of public corruption. One of the most galling revelations of his trial was that early in November of 2005 (less than two and a half months after the storm), he and his entire family flew on a city contractor's private jet to Jamaica and spent most of a week at a seaside condo as the contractor's guest. His explanation was that he was stressed and needed a break. What about the rest of the hundreds of thousands of your constituents who were more than stressed, some of them homeless, and fighting with government bureaucracy to try to rebuild their lives? You think *you* were stressed, Ray? As of this writing, Nagin is spending ten years as the guest of the federal government at the Texarkana prison camp. I hope he enjoys the free accommodations in Texarkana as much as he did those in Jamaica.

How is it that so many private citizens who run for office on the platform of being an outsider and fixing corruption get caught up in the same thing over and over again? Is our government—at all levels—such a cistern of corruption that even noble-minded people can't resist? Or are they all lying about being nobly minded?

• • •

Slowly, business came rolling in, starting with that quarter-million-dollar check in my home mailbox. We were doing better than most, as a result of our brand. Yet I was hesitant to move into an office and take on real hiring. In the years after Katrina, businesspeople lived in perpetual fear that no matter how well things were going, we were always waiting for the other shoe to drop. We worked at the dining room table much longer than we needed to, but we were building cash reserves to have a safety net in case there was an aftershock.

In early 2008, we finally moved back downtown into an office and hired an intern to help us manage our rapidly growing workload. I love interns. You have to find young people who genuinely want to engage in the business and learn about it, rather than those who just need college credit. Those who are genuinely interested will be an asset to the team—not just a drain on everyone's time. While most colleges set the expectation that internships are unpaid, we always pay our interns. This places you higher up in the list of priorities in their world, and you are less likely to have them miss a big project due to a fraternity or sorority party. The best part is that it is a low-cost, low-risk get-to-know-you. If they like the company and do a great job, you can look to hire them when they graduate. If not, then you end the relationship on good terms and move along. Erin Schrepfer landed in the former category. When she graduated, we gave her a full-time position, and she worked for us for over five years as an account manager before continuing on in a successful career in the hospitality industry.

Everybody Was Going through Something

While we were busy fighting client perceptions and trying to win business for the city, it's important to note that most people were still fighting personal battles at the same time. They were fighting with insurance companies, managing contractors, living in a FEMA trailer, or getting adjusted to a new home in a new town with a new school district and new neighbors—everybody had something major that they were working through outside of work. It was so common that you didn't even talk much about these challenges any longer; you just presumed that the person you were talking to was going through some kind of *something*.

It was a unique time in the history of competitive business in the New Orleans hospitality industry. Everybody was in it together—hotels, suppliers, competitors, and tourism promotion entities. The mind-set was that it didn't matter *who* got the business, as long as we got business to New Orleans. In the long run, we knew that would lead to more business overall, and everyone would eventually get their share. To an extent, that feeling carries on to this day, and I think we are all better for it.

One of many examples of this collaboration jumps to mind. A major meeting planning company held their annual client event in New Orleans. This brought 1,200 travel planners and their clients to the city, which was a wonderful opportunity to showcase all that we have to offer. At the last minute, they notified the Convention and Visitors Bureau that they needed sponsors for three dinners of 1,200 people each. *Thirty-six hundred free meals!* And of course it had to be top-quality New Orleans cuisine; we could not feed them po'boy sandwiches. So the Convention Bureau called the top three DMCs in to a meeting to see what we could do. Each one of us took a night and coordinated with our restaurants, caterers, and venues to get the sponsorship to put on three very memorable events. Knowing what I know about the competitive situation in other cities, I am hard-pressed to imagine this happening anywhere but New Orleans.

· · ·

With the benefit of full hindsight, it's also amazing to see that good things really do come out of bad. While it doesn't make the bad any easier to handle, it does offer hope going forward.

Prior to Katrina, the public school system in New Orleans was an unmitigated catastrophe. Of the low percentage of students who did graduate, most were hopelessly unprepared for college or any type of entry-level career. It wasn't just the terrible education; many of the schools lacked the basics—like functioning water fountains and bathrooms. Anybody who could, mortgaged the farm to send their children to private school. Many others moved to the far suburbs, enduring endless commutes so their children could go to adequate schools.

The city's school board itself was a cesspool of corruption, serving as a money spigot for the family of Congressman William "Dollar Bill" Jefferson, among many others. Jefferson's eighteen-year career in Washington ended when he was sent to the federal pen on corruption charges unrelated to the school board—but aided significantly by the $90,000 in marked bills they found in his freezer. The rest of his family ended up in prison on school board–related corruption charges.

After Katrina, the state took over the school district and, lacking the ability to rebuild it from the state level, turned the schools over one by one to charter school operators. What resulted was the first all-charter school district in the country. As a result, graduation rates are up by twenty points and test scores are up by over twenty-five points. The physical quality of the schools is back up to standard, which has greatly reduced the obstacles to learning.

It is funny how the people who should be most interested in student achievement are so vehemently opposed to charter schools. It just shows you that the teachers' unions and the activist members are more interested in collecting union dues than advancing education in the inner cities of this country. Thankfully, there are a lot of success stories like the one in New Orleans, and the public is beginning to understand it.

I mentioned the volunteers who descended on New Orleans in the years after Katrina. Church groups, school groups, corporate groups, and volunteers of every stripe came here to help. They rebuilt schools, homes, and parks; gave out food and water to people working on their own homes; and contributed in many other ways. There is no official count, but the number of people has to be in the hundreds of thousands, and the volunteer hours in the millions. The impact on the pace of recovery cannot be underestimated.

I met numerous people who took their entire year's vacation time to come volunteer. Then they took the money they had saved to spend on that vacation and donated it to the recovery. One couple from Minnesota I met on a Habitat for Humanity home-build project had been here three times in a year and a half! It opens your eyes to the true goodness of people and the American spirit, and also makes you ask yourself, "Am I doing my part to help out my fellow man?" I think I do, but many of these people set a pretty high bar.

A City Transforms

Prior to Katrina, a big portion of the New Orleans economy centered on the tourism and hospitality industry, which employed more than 70,000 people. The port is also a huge contributor to the economy, and we have substantially more lawyers than seem necessary for a city this size. But beyond that, the economy was not particularly diversified. The offshore oil and gas industry still had a role, but a lot of those jobs moved to Houston (low taxes, friendly government—go figure). So you had this really vibrant hospitality economy and this fairly stodgy port/law/oil side and not much in between.

An interesting confluence of events took place to change all of that. A lot of young people were among those who came down with the various volunteer groups to do work after the storm. And with the remaking of the education system, New Orleans became a magnet for organizations like Teach for America, where recent grads commit to a couple of years of teaching in an underserved area. It is sort of the Millennial version of the Peace Corps. When the Recession hit, the job market for recent college graduates shrank considerably. Many of these folks looked for someplace where they could do some good while waiting for the job market to turn around. New Orleans offered that opportunity.

A lot of the young people who came to help out ended up liking it here. The music, arts, and cool vibe that make the city great for visitors were equally compelling to this group, and the word quickly spread. What followed was an astronomic growth of new technology businesses run by twentysomethings. The economic leaders of the city quickly caught on to this, and investment groups, incubators, and other support systems quickly sprang up. The state came up with incentives to lure digital-economy businesses to locate here, and it wasn't long before *Forbes* magazine named New Orleans the "#1 Brain Magnet" in America.

What followed was a complete makeover of the downtown landscape. Young people want to live in the heart of the city, so dozens of largely vacant office buildings that had been floundering since the oil bust of the eighties were renovated into apartments, condos, and mixed-use developments.

New restaurants, grocery stores, and retail followed. We now have a thriving scene in the Central Business District that previously was mostly empty after 5:00 p.m. It's a lot of fun to be around—even if I am the oldest person in the elevator of my building each morning.

. . .

As 2007 turned into 2008, there was a growing sense of optimism that the city had turned a corner. It was surely *different,* and change always bothers some people, especially the old guard. But most people were so happy about the contrast between the present and the previous two years that even though nothing was back to the way we lived prior to August 25, 2005, it felt a lot like success. Little did we know what was just around the bend.

CHAPTER EIGHT

BLOODBATH AND SETBACK: THE GREAT RECESSION

*"Well, Jane, it just goes to show you. It's always
something. If it ain't one thing, it's another."*

—ROSEANNE ROSEANNADANNA

Three years had passed since Katrina, and things were moving in the right direction. Business was picking up, the city looked much like itself (but newer!), and people had settled into their lives. But a new storm was brewing far out of the sight of anyone who was not a part of the financial world.

I actually had a little preview of what was coming. When I refinanced my house in 2004 (one of three times that I did this to put money into the business between 1999 and 2004), I was told that as a business owner it would be better to do a "low doc" or "stated income" loan. Most small-business owners don't take an official salary that is reported on W-2 forms; they use the profits of the business as their income. Without a W-2 salary, banks get nervous. I knew I could support the new payments, so I didn't really care, but I remember questioning the mortgage company about this process. "You just sign a form telling them what you make" was their answer. This seemed very odd to me and a little too easy, and I still remember the conversation. What kind of bank would just take your word about your income? I wasn't lying about my income, so it didn't really matter to me at the time, but it stuck out as being hard to believe.

Sure enough, people all over the country were getting "low doc" or "stated income" loans, and a lot of them were greatly exaggerating their income and taking out mortgages well beyond their means. As we know, the chickens came home to roost in 2008, when the mortgage market collapsed, and a number of large financial institutions went bankrupt or required huge government bailouts—triggering the Great Recession.

This hit the corporate events and incentive industry particularly hard. When it was reported that AIG hosted a lavish incentive event at a five-star resort just as they accepted a bailout from the federal government, corporate events and incentives were suddenly in the spotlight. The perception was that corporate executives were spending money on swanky parties while their shareholders suffered.[8] Suddenly the press and activists were sweeping high-end hotels, checking the readerboards to see which companies were hosting events at the hotels. The bad press was overwhelming. President Obama made a speech in which he said that in light of the current events, nobody should be having "boondoggles in Las Vegas." This threw a wet cloth on an already bad situation.

Corporate meetings and incentive programs were canceled en masse. Even healthy companies that were not part of the financial system collapse cut out their events, fearing the optics. Layoffs were rampant throughout the industry, with many of my client companies cutting 50 percent or more from their meeting-planning departments. The whole fiasco became known as the "AIG Effect."

Studies indicate that in-person events have the greatest return on investment of any marketing activity except a firm's own website. The opportunity to spend quality time with your best customers (which is what was happening at the AIG event) through events and incentive travel programs is a key part of maintaining long-term relationships. But that all took a backseat to the immense amount of bad press.

So there we were, barely three years out from Katrina, and our entire industry had come to a crashing halt. This is one of the ulcer-inducing inevitabilities of being an entrepreneur: You can build a great com-

---

8   Subsequent research done by the incentive company that produced the AIG event showed that its shareholders received an ROI on that particular event in excess of 300 percent.

pany, have a great team, be on an amazing growth pace, and something completely unrelated to your business happens and you suffer a major setback. I joke now that I have been through three events that have completely stopped my business—9/11, Katrina, and the Great Recession. If I have survived all of that and still stayed in business (and some would say successfully), then they can throw anything at me, and I will always make it. Nothing can knock me down for long.

While I credit some of my success to having acquired an inordinate amount of resilience, there is more to the picture. If you leave a corporate job to start your own business and it doesn't go well, people will give you a pass and welcome you back into the workforce. But once you have been an entrepreneur for ten years, you are basically unemployable. Employers know that you are used to doing things your own way, and they fear you may jump right back into starting another company as soon as the opportunity presents itself. Entrepreneurs are, without a shadow of a doubt, guilty of wanting to do things their own way, and it is a matter of time before they don't fit back in with the corporate world. So while I could have used any of these events as a reason to throw in the towel and get a steady job, I knew that wasn't going to work. So there was no choice but to press on.

About a year into the fallout from the financial collapse, there was no end in sight, and resources were starting to run low. We began to look for opportunities to diversify outside our immediate industry. We found out that the Avis car rental company was looking for an operator for their downtown New Orleans location. The way this arrangement works is that you are not an employee of Avis, nor do you own the location. It is essentially a management contract that you are awarded to operate the location. Where most of the airport locations are operated by Avis corporate, the downtown and suburban locations are managed by Agency Operators. Avis owns all of the capital costs—primarily the cars, the building, and the land—and the Agency Operator is responsible for the operating costs. A percentage of the revenues is deposited into the operator's bank account on a monthly basis. So there were minimal start-up costs, very few fixed costs, and a steady stream of income. My kind of business model!

We applied and went through a fairly rigorous screening process. Avis was particularly impressed with our network of hotel contacts, as there was an untapped opportunity to generate referrals from hotel concierge desks. We were awarded the contract to operate the downtown New Orleans location, and Terry moved over to the Avis complex to run this operation. This took the pressure off our cash flow. While we weren't getting rich doing it, it was enough to cover Terry's salary, plus a little, and spare PRA that expense. We eventually were awarded another location across the lake in Mandeville and operated both successfully for a number of years. The lesson here is this: Keep an eye on your marketplace, and when something impacts it, look for solutions before you find yourself in a crisis situation. PRA New Orleans did just that, and we were one of the only DMCs that didn't lay anybody off during the Recession.

· · ·

At some point in the mid-2000s, Patti Roscoe decided it was time to retire. She quietly shopped the company, and a deal was reached with a European DMC named Allied International, which had seven offices across Europe and in the Middle East. It was owned by a man named Jim Hensley, who became CEO of the combined companies, which were rebranded as AlliedPRA. The acquisition closed in November of 2007. At the time, it was reported that PRA had $79 million in annual revenue. Now, people have said a lot of negative things about Jim Hensley, and they may be substantiated, but one thing that is not arguable is that in this particular instance, he was the victim of horrific timing. Researchers say the beginning of the economic crisis began in December of 2007, just one month after Jim bought the company. Within a year, the global financial system had collapsed and the corporate meeting, event, and incentive industry collapsed too. Needless to say, Jim had taken out debt for the acquisition based on the cash flow that comes from a $79 million company, and a year later, he had a company generating less than half of that. You don't have to be a financial whiz to see the problem here. I can't hold Jim at fault for this. Nobody in our industry saw this coming. In 2009, Jim sold the whole company to the London-based private equity firm Core Capital.

By that time, everyone in the industry was circling the wagons. Layoffs were rampant, both among my peers and my clients in the meeting-planning business. Five-star hotels were dropping the word "Resort" from their names to try to lure businesses back who didn't want the stigma of appearing to do business at a property with a luxurious-sounding name. It was a bloodbath—across the board. Picking up the Avis business stopped the bleeding for us, but the Recession cost us two years of growth coming off the back of the three years of growth we lost after Katrina. We were overdue for a break.

CHAPTER NINE

ANOTHER DISASTER: BP AND THE DEEPWATER HORIZON EXPLOSION

"The harder you work, the luckier you get."

—GARY PLAYER

Sometime in the fall of 2009, I received a call from a client whose company was a preferred partner of AlliedPRA. "Hi, Jeff," she said, "I have a group coming to New Orleans, but they don't have the budget for a DMC."

This is the dreaded opening line for any DMC person. It is basically telling you that they want to take advantage of your years of experience and expertise in the city and not compensate you for it. It happens *all the time*. I don't know of any other industry that is expected to give out free advice like ours is. There is usually the promise of, "If you help me with this, I will bring you a good group down the road." But the ever-looming "good group" never seems to materialize. In any case, she needed some restaurant recommendations, and I politely gave them to her, fully expecting never to hear from her again.

One morning in late April of 2010, I was driving to work when a call came through on my cell from a number I didn't recognize. I didn't answer, but a message was left, so out of curiosity, I checked the message. "Hi, Jeff, this is Sharon. You helped me out with some free advice last fall, and I need to see if you can help me with something urgently."

On April 20, 2010, the Deepwater Horizon drilling rig in the Gulf of Mexico was operating in 5,100 feet of water approximately forty-one miles off the coast of Louisiana. The well was majority owned and operated by

BP. At 9:45 p.m., a methane leak in the drill line made its way up to the rig platform, where it ignited and caused a massive explosion. Eleven people were incinerated. Their bodies were never found. Rig workers jumped from high off of the rig platform into the sea below, trying to save themselves, and sustained serious injuries. It was horrific.

It wasn't until two days later that crews searching for the missing workers noticed a plume of oil coming up from below the surface of the water. What wasn't noticed at first was that the explosion had severed the drill pipe just at the point where it entered the seafloor, and immense quantities of oil were pouring out of the well 5,100 feet below the surface of the water. Sixty-two thousand barrels of oil per day were flowing out of this hole. Nobody in the world knew how to cap an oil leak at this depth. Nobody seemed to have ever thought about it, in spite of the proliferation of deepwater drilling operations around the world. The initial attempts to stop the leak were comically ineffective.

When I called Sharon back, I had no idea what to expect. BP had set up a command station with the Coast Guard at the Mobile Convention Center in Alabama. Sharon's company was there and was responsible for setting up hotel rooms for all of the people coming in to the command center. They had taken over the two large Renaissance hotels downtown and a few smaller hotels near the convention center. However, on the upcoming weekend, the Southeastern Conference was having a big athletic tournament there, and all of the hotel rooms had been committed to it, so Sharon had been tasked with moving a couple of thousand people from the four-star Renaissance properties to a smattering of Super 8s, Clarions, and the like in the suburbs. These people were already under a lot of stress from the situation they were working in, so their move *had* to go well. Sharon didn't think the bus company she was working with in Mobile was up to the task. Could I help? Well, the answer is always *YES!* in my world. I had less than forty-eight hours to put together a fleet of buses and a team of people to pull this operation off. By noon, I was driving to Mobile to meet Sharon and assess the situation. I spent the entire two-hour drive lining up buses and people.

The operation was a success: We got all of the people back to their downtown hotels after the weekend, and I headed back to New Orleans with my team. It was a jolt of adrenaline in an otherwise slow period. I fully expected that was the end of it.

• • •

May 23, 2010, was a Sunday, and the day before my forty-fourth birthday. I was playing golf at the Audubon Park Golf Club, a par-62 muni located five minutes from my house that is frequented by a lot of the neighborhood guys. I normally prefer the regulation courses, but some of the Fat Harry's regulars have a standing tee time on Sundays, and occasionally I join them. This was one of those days. Between the ninth and tenth holes, my phone rang. By now, I had her name saved in the phone: It was Sharon.

President Obama had ordered all available Coast Guard personnel to New Orleans starting the next day. It was such a hurried mobilization that the men and women of the Guard were not even told what their orders would be. They were told only to report to New Orleans within forty-eight hours for further instructions. Sharon told me they would begin arriving the next day, and she needed a shuttle system set up to pick them up at the airport and get them to hotels and then on to their assignment. I asked the obvious questions:

"How many are coming?"

"I don't know."

"Where are they going when they get here?"

"I don't know."

"Where do we take them next?"

"I don't know."

I stopped with the questions. We were to set up a staffing desk at 7:00 a.m. at the Crowne Plaza Airport hotel and have buses at the ready to transfer the incoming Coast Guard members . . . details to follow as they became available.

I finished up the round of golf, and over post-round beers at Fat

Harry's, I began making arrangements. First, I called Ed Sakakeeny, the owner of Carey Limousine. Carey had a fleet of minicoaches that I figured would give us more flexibility than full-size motor coaches. "Ed, I need a minimum of four minicoaches at the Crowne Plaza Airport at 7:00 a.m. tomorrow—until further notice. I may need more than that, but I won't know until I get there." Ed asked the same questions I had asked: How many are coming? Where are they going? When do they get here? Where do we take them next? And I gave him the same answers Sharon had given to me: I don't know. I told him what I did know, and Ed sent the buses. Next I called Kim Massicot, one of our go-to transportation staff. "Kim, I need to set up a desk at the Crowne Plaza Airport to manage a shuttle beginning at 7:00 a.m. tomorrow morning. I don't know how many people are coming or how long it will last. We'll figure that out when we get there. Can you be there?" Kim said sure and started asking all of the same questions. I had all of the same answers: "I don't know." She stopped asking and we agreed she would see me in the morning. We had no idea what was ultimately in store.

The Coast Guard set up a command center at the Crowne Plaza. We were to meet the incoming Guard members at the airport and bring them to the Crowne Plaza, where they would be given an assignment and a hotel room for the night. We would take them to their accommodations, utilizing a handful of hotels around the New Orleans airport. Their assignment would be a function of their training. If they were fully certified in oil-spill operations, we would take them to one of a number of operational hubs along the Gulf Coast—depending on their specialties and the current needs. If they required further training, we would take them back and forth each day to the Michoud facility in New Orleans East, where they would train for three to six days and then get deployed. The command-center staff had no idea who was coming in each day, so everything had to be processed and set up on the fly as the people came in. As we handled their hotel assignments, there were some additional nuances to deal with. They were all in double-occupancy rooms, but needless to say, men and women couldn't be assigned together. In addition, no serviceperson was required to bunk with someone of a lower rank. We had to track who came and left each day and make room assignments accordingly. The hotel tracked the names after we made the assignments, but they ultimately just cleaned all the rooms every day, while handling some combination of staying-on and arriving guest services.

As you might be able to imagine, it was chaos. In addition to dealing with unknown amounts of personnel and destinations every day, we had no budget and no method for getting paid—not even a contract. After a couple of weeks, I finally drew up a contract and sent it to Sharon, but it never did get approved. She was being pulled in a million directions, and I was only one part of the process. In a month's time, BP quickly owed us several hundred thousand dollars, which in turn, I owed to Carey and the staff that had been on the job sixteen hours a day from the beginning. Sharon eventually was able to set up a process where they would pay weekly with a one-time American Express card. She was wonderful at getting my invoices approved in a timely manner once this was set up, but I did have to impress on her the urgency of making this happen. We were a small company and certainly couldn't bankroll this operation for any significant time.

Off to the Redneck Riviera

After a week or so of all this, I went on my annual trip to the beach at Gulf Shores, Alabama, for Memorial Day with a group of friends from New Orleans. Gulf Shores is on the Gulf of Mexico near the Florida border. It's famous for its beautiful white-sand beaches and is accurately nicknamed the "Redneck Riviera" due to the clientele it draws from the southeast USA. Nonetheless, it is a very nice beach and the closest one to New Orleans. We always set up shop in a condo tower a couple of doors down from the Flora-Bama Lounge, which sits exactly on top of the border between Florida and Alabama. For years, the liquor laws regulating everything from drinking age to closing times were different in the two states. There literally was a line painted down the middle of the building, and people would dutifully move to the Florida side of the line when closing time hit in Alabama.

The Flora-Bama really defies description: It is a combo beach bar/redneck dive/music hall dating from the mid-1960s. It became famous back in the eighties when it instituted its annual "Mullet Toss" as a way to drive business during the slow spring season between when the snowbirds leave and the summer vacationers arrive. A mullet is a trash fish native to the Southeast that proliferates due to the fact that it is completely inedible. I don't even know that other fish will eat it. If you ever see one with its long, skinny body, you'll know why that tail that you see coming down from the back of the heads of many fashion-challenged Southern men is known as a "mullet." At the Flora-Bama, the annual Interstate Mullet Toss is a two-day competition where dead mullets are thrown across the state line. And this is just the tip of the iceberg when it comes to the shit that goes on in this place. Jimmy Buffett and Kenny Chesney are regulars. You never know what's going to happen—but whatever does will certainly be decidedly lowbrow. And awesome.

• • •

On Sunday as I was on the way down to the beach, I got a call from Sharon. The Coast Guard had just announced a big move of people starting Monday and Tuesday, and she couldn't get in touch with the bus company in Mobile. Could I take care of it? I told her I would get something there. Now think about this: It is *Sunday* of Memorial Day weekend, and most of New Orleans is at the beach, just like us, or at fishing camps, or somewhere—but they're certainly not answering phones. I eventually got the dispatcher from one of our motor coach companies on his cell, and then he had to track down drivers who would answer the phone on a holiday weekend and mobilize them over to Alabama. I got in touch with a couple of the key staff who had worked the previous Mobile job and got them on the road. Sharon organized hotel rooms for them in Mobile, and we were off and running again. One of the key benefits of working with a Destination Management Company is the local connections we have, and this is a perfect example. Being able to get in touch with whomever is needed, at any time of the day or night, is a big value that we bring to our clients. Over the years, the number of people I have had to track down to get help for a client after hours is too many to count. I have roused everyone from the owners of bus companies to the general manager of FedEx—and many, many bars and restaurants—to help clients with last-minute requests. Try doing that via Google, meeting planners!

Back in New Orleans, things were as chaotic as could be. In addition to the logistics center at the Crowne Plaza at the airport, a command center had been set up in Houma, and we were asked to staff it. Houma, Louisiana, is the closest city of any size (and it is not that big) to Port Fourchon, the main departure point for the supply ships and helicopters going out into the Gulf. There are a handful of Best Western and Holiday Inn–type hotels there, and Sharon had contracted them all for BP and our Coast Guard. We had to staff someone down there to handle the hotel logistics. It was an impressive setup—the number of computers and monitors rivaled anything you would see at NASA—and there were large-screen monitors live streaming the oil pouring out of the ocean floor. Our desk was in the corner of a back room next to one of Sharon's people. I sent one of the guys who had worked the Mobile job down there at first, but it was close quarters, and after a couple of weeks of twelve hours a day, the personalities were not working out. Sharon asked me to make a change. Actually, she told me to—by the following day.

• • •

I met Christie Drury through a mutual friend in the industry, and she had started to do contract operations work for us. Young, attractive, and engaging, she was also not afraid of work, and she put in a lot of hours. I asked her to help out with the Houma desk . . . beginning . . . like, *now*. She was working at night helping to run her father's beach volleyball complex,

Coconut Beach, so she was in the unique position of being available and flexible. I thought she was a good candidate who would not rub anyone the wrong way, which was a key requirement of this job in this location. Christie turned out to be a perfect fit and manned the Houma operation for the next four months.

Meanwhile, our transportation operation was beginning to tax the system. Once the Coast Guard arrived at the Crowne Plaza, they would be processed in and then given their assignments for the next day—training, field operations, et cetera. It was taking until ten o'clock at night for us to know how many people were going to each location the next day, starting at 7:00 a.m. Ed at Carey Limousine was having to keep buses and drivers on hold each night until we gave them the details for the next day. For a few weeks this was sustainable, but it was starting to take a toll on his operation as we realized this whole situation was not going to be ending any time soon. I worked on Sharon while Kim worked on the people on the ground to finally get a commitment to have this information to us by 7:00 p.m. each day, which made Carey's job a bit easier. But even this took a lot of work, and with all of the things going on and all of the pressure on BP and its contractors, we were simply not a priority. However, we all knew that the minute a bus was not where it was supposed to be, the result would be catastrophic. This was just one example of the logistical challenges we faced as the scope of this job turned from weeks into months.

As the operation kept going with no end in sight—and the video of oil pouring out of the seabed never stopped—we faced another challenge: competition. In the beginning, we were flying under the radar, but as time went on, people noticed that we had become a major player in the transportation operation. There was another shuttle system being run in downtown New Orleans by one of BP's corporate contractors, and of course, the one in Mobile as well. Both of these companies were using their corporate contacts at BP to try to wrestle the business away from us. I was in constant conversations with Sharon—usually after the dinner hour—assuring her that I was proving the value in what we were providing. She was happy with our operation, but the reality of corporate politics is that someone could easily pull rank and give the job to one of *their* cronies, so I wanted to be sure she had all the ammunition needed to justify our relationship. We were fighting battles on multiple fronts, with the logistics, the competition, and keeping staff and suppliers happy and motivated. I'd be lying if I said it didn't shave a couple of years off me.

Our billing was in excess of $100,000 a week, so it was no surprise that competitors were sniffing around. The amount of money BP was throwing at the overall operation was enormous. The worldwide press was all over them on a daily basis, and rightly so. It was a terrible tragedy and the largest environmental disaster in history. But I have to take issue with the often-repeated notion that they were not doing enough about it at the time. They spent billions of dollars and spared no cost to try to find a solution. It is just that the situation was unprecedented, and off-the-shelf solutions didn't exist. What you can fault them for is that if you have drilling operations worldwide at 5,000-plus feet below sea level, somebody should have had an emergency plan—they didn't. But once the catastrophe happened, they threw every resource available at the problem.

A lot of local people did well as a result of the tragedy, which was one of the unnoticed effects of this kind of situation. Certainly my company and Carey did quite well. Still in the final stage of the Great Recession, both our staff and the drivers had been underworked for a long time. Every time I spoke with a driver at the operation, they thanked me profusely for bringing the work to them. I had friends who popped up catering operations out in the field to feed the thousands of people working in the cleanup effort, far from any restaurants or stores. The list goes on. The work needed doing, and we all did what needed to be done.

There were a few interesting sidebars to all this that didn't get covered in the press, or at least not noticeably. Having lived through Katrina and her aftereffects, and the major story of 2010, which was the BP oil spill, I have some insight into the contrast between what is said in the press and what is the reality on the ground. It is striking. Bad news sells, and the other side of the issues doesn't get nearly the coverage. I find the "Corrections" sections in news outlets particularly comical. A headline can be blazed across the front page or the top of a news site one day, and when it turns out to be wrong, the correction appears in small print somewhere deep in the paper or website. They should be required to print the corrections in the same place and in the same font in which the erroneous story was originally placed.

But, back to the sidebars. It was widely concluded that the seafood industry in the Gulf of Mexico would be devastated by the spill. All fishing operations were closed down by the federal government, putting thousands of fishermen, shrimpers, and oystermen out of work. They were eventually compensated handily by BP as part of the settlement with state and local governments, but at the time, there was plenty of uncertainty. Many of them devoted their boats and time as part of the cleanup effort, replacing fishing income with cleanup income. It was a trade-off nobody was happy to make, for sure. There were extensive studies on the seafood harvested from the Gulf for many years, testing to see if it was tainted from the effects of the oil spill. In every case, there was not even a remote impact on the safety of Gulf seafood. Turns out, fish can swim. When conditions are not optimal in a location, they swim to a better location. For years, news headlines would say, "Such and such a study is taking place on the safety of Gulf seafood," with the obvious implication that something was wrong. People made judgments based on that type of news and made buying decisions based on it, when the reality was that the fish were fine. The same type of reporting that was harming the meeting and convention business years after Katrina hurt our fishing industry years after the oil spill.

Oysters from Texas and Oil from Everywhere

One industry that did suffer was the oyster harvest, but not for the reasons people think. In an effort to keep the oil slick offshore, water from the Mississippi River was diverted from its normal path and sent careening through the bays and inshore areas where the prime oyster beds reside. This infusion of freshwater into their normal, saltier ecosystem killed oyster beds across the region. People in Louisiana love oysters, and the fact that we had to eat oysters from Texas was one of the more painful outcomes of this ordeal.

One other interesting thing that was revealed as a result of the spill is that oil is ever-present in the waters of the Gulf of Mexico, whether there is drilling or not. Oil seeps naturally from the floor of the Gulf. At the time of the spill, reports of tar balls under the sand of the beaches of Florida and Alabama devastated the summer business for those beach communities. The majority of planned vacationers canceled their stays because they were in fear of a huge oil slick coming up on the beach while they were there. This certainly was not an unreasonable precaution, since at the beginning of summer, nobody had any idea how this would play out. While some of the oil found on Gulf beaches could be tied to the spill, the origin of the vast majority could not be determined one way or the other. Much of it would have been there anyway, as the oil—which occurs naturally—works its way up to the floor of the Gulf and every other body of water that has oil beneath it.

In all, our operations went on from May 24 through the end of October, moving hundreds of Coast Guard personnel every day for close to five months. The oil flowed uninterrupted into the Gulf of Mexico for eighty-seven days with a total of 130 million gallons pouring out. The well was finally successfully capped on July 15, but the cleanup effort continued in full force for months after. We began to slow down the number of people we were moving daily in mid-September, and the whole operation wound down in the third week of October.

Most of our industry was still suffering from the Recession, but we had experienced a jolt of adrenaline, business, and, importantly, money. It was an E-ticket ride by any measure.

CHAPTER TEN

KEEPING IT ALL TOGETHER

"Success is where preparation and opportunity meet."

—BOBBY UNSER

A t this time, our competition was still suffering and, in many cases, still cutting back. With our fresh injection of funds, I saw an opportunity to get ahead of our competitors while they were down.

The first thing I did was hire Christie Drury to a full-time position. She had dutifully manned the remote outpost of Houma without complaint for nearly four months, and I had seen her in action at her father's beach volleyball complex slinging drinks, cleaning the grill, mopping floors— whatever it took. She was always smiling and happy while at it. This is the kind of person I like to hire. There are people of every generation— it's not just the Millennials—who expect the world to be handed to them without the commensurate amount of effort on their part. In the type of lean operations I prefer to run, there is no room for people who are not contributing 120 percent. If you can clean a grill and smile, you will fit in just fine with me.

I put Christie into a sales manager role, starting her out focusing on hotel relationships and quickly moving her into handling some of our national clients. She was fantastic at everything she touched and became well respected throughout the AlliedPRA system.

I also quickly invested in some industry trade shows and events that we wouldn't have done otherwise, in an effort to spread our reach as far as possible while everyone else couldn't get out in front of clients. Of course, if the client doesn't have any business yet, neither of you will see an immediate return. But the relationships we developed during this time paid off down the road. You have to be willing to invest in your business, regardless of the immediate return, making smart and targeted investments for the long term. In my business, investments are not in material inputs; invested money is best spent on getting out in front of potential clients and building relationships.

• • •

Throughout 2010, another story was playing out. My mother had suffered a stroke a few years earlier, and that, along with years of heavy smoking and drinking, had caught up with her. She had gone voluntarily into a nursing home but was now spending most of her time in the hospital, with regular stints in the intensive care unit. Esophageal cancer had taken away her ability to speak, so our conversations were held on paper. She was still very alert, but mostly bedridden and dependent on morphine and the other drugs they were giving her.

My sister and brother didn't have the ability to make frequent visits, so I started going up to Kingston every couple of weeks to support Mom and report back to the family. She had signed a power of attorney after her stroke, so I took over her affairs and kept everything in order and her finances out of the hands of her manipulative boyfriend. This slug was a hoarder of the highest order and had destroyed her house. I expected he would use this opportunity to clean her out, so I took protective measures to shield her assets.

The trips were not fully sad affairs, since I reconnected with a number of high school friends who still lived in Kingston and I spent quality time with my father and Sally, my stepmother. I always stayed with Mama Rose, and she was always happy to have her "Irish son" back in her house.

I was optimistic that Mom would recover, and when she was in the nursing home, I took her out of her room and wheeled her around the grounds, telling her that she would be better soon. She always agreed and expressed optimism to my face. I was oblivious to the signs that she had actually long since given up. Looking back, I see them now, but my natural optimism, combined with her BS-ing, kept me in the dark at the time. Just before Christmas, the doctor called a family meeting. I was there in person along with Dad, and Susan and David joined on the phone. There was nothing further to be done medically, and they recommended a hospice situation. I had heard the term hospice thrown around before, but until that day, I never fully understood its meaning. The doctor and nurse were very compassionate, but they were quite clear that this was it. It would be best to send her back to the nursing home, forgo further medical attention, and make her as comfortable as possible while she waited to die. I looked her in the eye and asked if she was on board with this. She had a tear in her eye but emphatically nodded yes.

Nancy Jean Howard O'Hara died peacefully on January 5, 2011, at the age of seventy-two. The manager of the nursing home called me that afternoon to let us know it was happening. In the course of sorting through it all, I had called my father to get his advice on some sibling friction about how to handle everything. He lived about an hour away from the nursing home, and unbeknownst to me at the moment, he had driven straight up and sat at her bedside until she passed away that evening. They had been divorced for thirty-five years at this point, but they had known each other since they were five years old, and that's just the kind of man he is.

• • •

Back at the office, I continued to hire, bringing in a couple of former college athletes. Erin Gremillion played soccer at the University of Louisiana at Lafayette, and Sarah Howard played volleyball at Loyola University in New Orleans. With their athletic backgrounds, they brought a competitive spirit to the team that I love.

I was excited that we were growing, but of course even growth doesn't come without incident. With the addition of Christie, Erin, and Sarah, it was clear to our existing staff that I was hiring a higher talent level now, and the staff felt threatened. I had thought there was a possibility that this might happen, but I hoped that people would step up to the challenge and elevate their own games. But not everyone could live with the competition, which is a natural effect in a growing company or a growing department. You have to be sensitive to your people who are in place, but you should *always* hire the very best people you can afford.

Another thing critical in hiring is that you have to hire people that you like to be around. Ask yourself if you would spend time with these people outside of work. That is an important litmus test to me. You are going to spend more time with your coworkers than your spouse in a typical week, and they have to be people that you look forward to seeing every day.

CUSTOMER SERVICE

One thing I have always had a fanatical focus on is impeccable customer service. It's just in my nature, for one thing. I love the hospitality business because you get so many opportunities to interact with your guests and *make them happy*. What other industry has such a focus on making people happy? And who doesn't like happy people?

Providing world-class service is a market differentiator, and it doesn't cost that much more than providing average service. Certainly our inputs and suppliers have to be of the highest quality, and that costs marginally more. But most of the value in great service is the effort the people put into it. If you are going to do something anyway, there is no reason not to command excellence in the process.

I've been exposed to some great champions of this philosophy, starting with Bob Foster at the Sheraton. And there were many others along the way. The general manager of the Grand Union Supermarket in Kingston had a blood-vessel-bursting pet peeve. If he ever found a loaded grocery cart abandoned in the front of the store, he would go absolutely off the rails.[9] I can still hear him to this day: "We spent all of

---

9   Presumably the customer had finished their shopping and then found the lines too long to wait to check out.

this money to get them to walk into the front door of the store and spent all of this time to get the right items on the shelves to meet their needs. They spent all of their effort to load their cart up with our goods, in our place of business, and now they are standing in front of the store, with their money in hand waving it at us, *and we aren't good enough to take their money from them*!!" His round face would be red as a beet, and the rant was verbatim every time. It is a good lesson: No matter how good 99 percent of your processes are, it takes just one breakdown in the chain to bring the whole system to a grinding, unprofitable halt.

Another voice I still hear in my head belongs to Mike Whipple, general manager of the Sheraton Inner Harbor. As a young manager, I was not alone in taking a righteous approach to guest service. I see it in my young managers today. If someone had a legitimate complaint, I would do anything possible to solve it. If they were trying to scam the system, I would resist. Eventually some of these complaints would make their way up to Mike Whipple's office. His response? "We spent a quarter of a million dollars (our marketing budget) to get these people in the door, and *you* are going to piss them off?" It's a lot more expensive to *get* a customer than to make them happy once you have them.

Because of the BP contract, I was able to get a bit ahead of the competition. Was it lucky? Maybe. But I believe you make your own luck. Being in the right place at the right time only works if you have already built the network and the expertise to make it happen. I had to walk a fine line between being persistent enough to keep the work coming and not being a pain in Sharon's butt with my phone calls and lobbying. I had to balance the fiscal responsibility to the client and keep costs down as much as possible—all the while being fair to my suppliers in order to ensure I had the equipment and people where I needed them each day. It was a tightrope on many levels, but it worked, and it set us up for the next chapter in our company's history.

Is It Time to Become a "Grown Up" Company?

This was a question I had been asking myself over and over. I had done a good job keeping overhead low, and the team was overperforming, definitely punching above their weight. But with a bit of honest self-examination, I saw more and more that my passion was in big-picture thinking. My interest in the small details was waning. Had the time come to build out the organization?

At this point, Terry was off running Avis, and it was just me as the leader of this growing team. My management philosophy is one of empowerment and accountability. I want people to make decisions. Part of growing is that sometimes people make the wrong decision, but I believe a wrong decision is better than no decision. That is how you learn and grow. Now, making the same wrong decision twice is another story. But I believe in giving people the tools to do their job and the courage to make decisions. As such, we don't have committees, and you already know how I feel about meetings. The independent thinkers who thrive in the DMC industry love this about me. But it does lead to a decided lack of structure, and there came a point when the team came to me and said they wanted more structure to our system.

There were some simmering personnel issues that they thought could be addressed by having a more defined playbook. And some kind of regular meeting would make it so that everybody knew what their teammates were working on. The meeting part was easy, but frankly, I didn't think I was the right person to implement structure in the organization. To do so would have required the commitment to follow it all the way through—and stick with it. I am more effective and have much more fun flying by the seat of my pants; it's just my nature. I wouldn't have been able to live up to the promise to institute and ensure the structure that my team needed, and I knew it. To quote Harry Callahan in *Magnum Force*, "A man's got to know his limitations."

I had been toying with the idea of creating a Director of Sales position and bringing in an established leader. But a couple of things were holding me back: (1) my aversion to overhead, and (2) my uncertainty about how the team would take it. Well, number two had just gotten solved, as this was the opening I needed to raise the issue. As for number one, I knew I could fund the position for a year with the cash on hand, and presumably by that point, the new person would be paying for themselves.

A lot of entrepreneurs might have a hard time ceding control of the daily operation, but I was actually comfortable with that part. I was looking forward to having some support with the day-to-day stuff so I could free up my time to look at the big picture.

Make a Mental Note: Face Your Fears

The lesson here is that every person has their strengths and their weaknesses. Sometimes they're not always apparent. But when things come up along the journey that make me uncomfortable or that I find I don't like dealing with, I make a mental note. I have to be able to break through that barrier or find a way to compensate for it. As an example, I have always been terrified of heights, so I decided I should take skydiving lessons to try to overcome my fear. The trouble is, if you are in a small, un-air-conditioned plane with fifteen other people, circling around to get to altitude, it gets *real* uncomfortable. I couldn't get out of the plane fast enough. Didn't cure anything.

As it turns out, it is ridiculously fun. You free-fall 10,000 feet over the course of sixty seconds and it is loud! The wind is rushing at 120 miles per hour, and there are all of these physical sensations. Then, when you pull the chute at 1,000 feet up, everything suddenly goes completely quiet, and you float to the ground. The contrast and accompanying rush of energy is beyond description.

My ongoing fear of heights aside, I am always on the lookout for things I don't like to do or don't feel that I am effective at. While many people try to put these things out of their mind, I look for solutions. Sometimes I can solve things internally; sometimes they are better solved with outside resources. In this case, I decided to take the risk, and I set out to hire someone to lead the team.

As an entrepreneur, when you are making a major hire, *always* retain a recruiting firm. Everyone knows that as the owner of the company, you have final decision-making power. But you need a layer in between you and the prospects. There may be applicants from competitors, suppliers, and even clients. You may not want to consider these candidates, but you also don't want to damage your relationship by being the one to say no. Effective initial screening will save you a lot of time. The recruiter can also reach out to people you want to target and maintain enough confidentiality to protect everyone. Finally, a recruiter will have the expertise to negotiate a compensation package that works for everyone. All of these things are potential sources of friction that are best handled by a third party.

I had a couple of people on my radar and had the recruiter reach out to them. One person who was definitely *not* on my radar was the Director of Sales at the Hyatt Regency, Cindy Hayes. She had been with Hyatt for thirty years, and I had met her when, a few years earlier, we interviewed with her to be Hyatt's in-house DMC when the hotel reopened after Katrina. She was definitely Ms. Corporate, and I was sure she wouldn't be able to fit in with the entrepreneurial climate of my company. I was more than surprised when she put her hat in the ring with the recruiter.

She did, however, possess a lot of qualities I liked. I gave the recruiter a list of reasons why she wouldn't like it at my company and instructed the recruiter to try and get her to self-eliminate. If she was still interested after that, I said, I would consider talking to her.

While hotels and DMCs are certainly closely related—we share the same clients and, of course, are part of the broader hospitality industry—the skill sets needed to be successful in each are very different. People from hotel backgrounds who come into the DMC business generally end up back in hotels. DMCs know this, but they still hire them in the hope that their hotel contacts will result in a fountain of new business. But at the end of the day, hotel sales is selling the same thing inside the same four walls every day. The number of rooms never changes, the amount of meeting space never changes. The rate parameters change a little based on season and booking pattern, but it's hardly a variety. That's why you see so many uninspired sales managers on hotel site inspection tours. How many times can you point out the new earthy colors in the guest rooms and still be enthused?

DMCs, on the other hand, have hundreds of venues, restaurants, excursions, entertainment, and themes at their disposal in every city. This is what makes the business exciting to the people who love it. Every client has different parameters and objectives, and we have to customize everything we do to fit each one of them. It truly means that every day is different. But to someone used to selling the same thing every day, it can also be rather daunting.

In the end, Cindy convinced the recruiter—and me—that she was ready for a change and could embrace the DMC industry. I will say that I did not make it easy on her to convince me. But her experience and organization skills were exactly the balance I needed to complement my modus operandi, so I decided to take the chance. Plus, she had been warned!

I am now happy to say that Cindy has worked out very well. As of this writing, she has been with us four-plus years and has been exactly what I needed to balance me out. There were certainly some growing pains, and as much as she worked to get ready for this culture, it is still a one-eighty from the "corporateness" of Hyatt. But we worked together, and she has embraced the culture and the business.

The team that grew into Inc. 5000 honorees was coming together. Katie Poche was working as one of our contract operations staff on Christie's recommendation, and she quickly proved herself to be a hard worker and a good leader. Plus, her University of Alabama education is a nice foil to all of the LSU fans in the office. A little conflict is always good to keep everything lively!

We brought Katie into a full-time entry-level role, and she quickly moved up the ranks to become a highly respected National Sales Manager. I like all of our salespeople to start out in operations and work their way up. Some of them end up loving operations and staying there. For the ones who make sales a career, I believe it is critical for them to understand the complex logistics that go into the operations of our events. No two days are the same; no two venues are the same. In order to create the events that achieve our clients' objectives, you have to know a lot more than the room capacity and type of food that is served. The Internet has made everyone an "expert," so we have to be the ones with the knowledge to guide our clients to great outcomes.

I also believe in pushing people past their comfort zone. I will give people responsibilities that they don't think they are ready for, but which I believe they can succeed in. Knowing that I believe in them pushes them to strive to succeed, and they always do! And once they achieve the success, I make a point to remind them that they didn't think they could do it—so that the next time I push them, they are likely to believe in themselves.

Having previously learned a lesson about hiring away from competitors, my philosophy has become firm: Bring in young, ambitious people and give them the tools to learn and be successful in their roles, while having a path to advancement and success. It has served all of us well. As we continue to grow, there will certainly be situations where this isn't always possible, but for me this is Option 1. It has produced a team of well-rounded, engaged, loyal, and passionate professionals that is highly regarded in our city and our industry. This philosophy also brings with it the added benefit of being able to watch people outperform their own expectations as they grow their careers. The personal satisfaction that goes along with that is the most rewarding aspect of my role.

The BP project was an opportunity for us, and I was able to leverage the success of it to dial up the next chapter of the company. As bad as the situation was in the Gulf, it provided a needed infusion for us at the most opportune time. The big question in my mind was, "Can we take full advantage?"

CHAPTER ELEVEN

SURVIVAL AND GROWTH

"Everyone wants to live on top of the mountain, but all of the happiness and growth occurs while you are climbing it."

—ANDY ROONEY

B y 2014, we were in a full-on growth stage. I had implemented some changes to our approach to business, and they were starting to pay off. Cindy had added the needed structure to the office and also gave me a sounding board with a different perspective. We added support staff who improved the productivity of the sales team and built out our contract operations staff. It was quite a change from the starts and stops before and after Katrina and before and after the Great Recession. But I am still paranoid and vigilant about the unknown next shoe to drop, and I surely always will be. In addition to my own personal success, there are many people whose livelihoods depend on the success of this business, and I am *terrified* of letting them down. The more we grow and the bigger we get, the more people who could be affected. That keeps me up at night, even in the best of times. The thing is, if I make a mistake that has some consequence, I can live with that. None of my calculated risks would threaten the life of the company. It is the events outside my control that worry me and are the most maddening when they happen. You can be doing fabulously, running a fantastic business with a great team, and something completely unrelated to you craters everything. Housing crisis anyone?

With that said, I have developed a high level of confidence in my resilience, and as I have said, I've been a business owner through 9/11, Hurricane Katrina, and the Great Recession, and I'm still in business. After surviving those disasters, I can't imagine anything else that could be thrown at me that would bring me down. Now is no different.

One of the changes that I implemented was to focus on who we wanted to take on as clients. An enormous amount of labor goes into creating a sales proposal for a client, and in many cases that cost isn't considered when the client looks at your value proposition. They look at what we charge for full service compared to what they can find on the Internet. Certain segments of the market are high maintenance and low margin, and others understand the value DMCs bring to the equation and understand the costs involved with that.

I made a decision to identify the market segments that understand our value and are willing to pay for it, and focus our sales efforts there. We would not pursue any players I identified as low margin, and, if they came looking for us, we would politely decline to bid on their business. It was amazing to me how many people actually got angry when we turned them down! The way I look at it, if I approach a provider and they tell me they don't want or can't take my business, they have saved us both time. But some people would actually argue about it!

What are some of the things that would trigger a TBNT (Thanks but No Thanks) response?

TBNT (THANKS BUT NO THANKS)

- **Including too many companies in your RFP.** The DMC business is a high-touch service business, and clients who know what they are looking for will do research before sending a request for proposal (RFP), narrowing it down to two or three companies at most that are the best potential fits for them.

- **Refusing to schedule a call to discuss your RFP.** Every event is unique, and the better we understand your goals and objectives, the better our proposal will be. If you can't take thirty minutes to discuss it with us, you are likely just shopping price.

- **An unrealistic budget.** This speaks for itself. We are a high-level service provider, and we will never be the low-cost provider in any bid situation. We are wasting our time with any work spent in the low end of the pool.

- **An unrealistic deadline to create a proposal.** If you really want a quality proposal, you have to understand the work that goes into providing that. If sufficient time is not provided, you either don't understand the process or don't respect our time. Either way, I am skeptical about attempting to work with you.

While these are somewhat specific to my business, the principles and the concept do translate across industries. A company can become vastly more profitable by focusing on its most profitable customers—*and* providing the high level of service the best customers require.

Salespeople hate saying no to anybody, and they naturally want to win every opportunity that comes in the door. But you have to get the team on board by showing them how the costs play out in the sales process and get them to buy in to the concept of saying no. The fact is, every minute they spend on a low-profit group is a minute they are not spending on a high-margin group. Your sales incentive plan should align with this exactly to ensure complete buy-in.

I read a great book called *The 1% Windfall* by Rafi Mohammed. Its simple premise is that if you improve your gross margin by one percent, you will increase your bottom line by twenty percent. Wow, that must be magic! A twenty-percent return just like that. And hey, a one-percent increase in gross margin seems achievable enough. *It actually is just about as simple as that.* Most businesses run about a five-percent net profit margin. Your fixed costs are, well, fixed, so by definition they stay the same regardless of your revenue level or gross margin. Any increase in gross margin, therefore, flows right to your bottom line. So if your typical net profit is five percent, an additional one percent is a twenty-percent increase in your net profit. Voilà!

We set about identifying ways that we could increase our gross margin without losing sales or compromising the customer experience. Any clients who feel they paid too much, but worked with you anyway, are not going to be happy. And there is a low chance that they will be repeat clients. Some of the services we provide are apples-to-apples with our competitors and have to be priced competitively. But other services require a lot of expertise and creativity, and people *should* pay more for our expertise. You wouldn't hire the lowest-cost divorce lawyer, would you?

There are also a lot of things that come up at the last minute on an event that require your DMC to pull off a miracle. It may not be so much a miracle as the years building up the contacts and expertise to be able to make things happen at the last minute. Surely we should be compensated for having developed this over many years. We spend a lot of time when we are not working on something specific to do our version of R&D, so that we always have resources available to service the unexpected. Certainly there is a billable value in that, too.

By taking a fresh look at how we charged for our services, we were able to add this 1%/20%, and I reinvested it into the business to further support our growth. And, of course, we revised our employee incentive system to support this goal.

Speaking of incentives, I want my team to focus on three things: total revenue, gross margin, and client satisfaction. Our incentive plan is focused on rewarding hitting benchmarks in each of these areas. There are a couple of key points to remember. The first is that you mustn't have too many goals. Research indicates that three goals is an optimal number; beyond that, people lose focus and don't get to any of them. The second is that your incentive plan must be closely aligned with the outcomes you are trying to achieve. Tying compensation to the outcomes you are working toward ensures focus on the most important metrics in the organization.

. . .

This leads to my philosophy on compensation in general. You are already clear on my aversion to overhead. However, any company in which the compensation is largely commission-based experiences high turnover. Turnover is expensive and painful. Some entrepreneurs like the internal competition and churning out the low performers, but not me. My preference is to hire well in the first place and give people opportunities. My objective is to pay a comfortable salary commensurate with each position, and then offer the opportunity to make a significant bonus that's achievable. On the base salary, I never want to have somebody worrying about not paying their rent if they don't hit their numbers in a month. I do want them to feel like they have skin in the game and will succeed when the company succeeds, so they can achieve a significant increase in pay for hitting objectives.

You also have to make the incentives achievable. I have seen far too many incentive plans that are pie in the sky, and people don't even try. Entrepreneurs will argue that you have to set the bar high. There's nothing wrong with that: Have another level of incentive for a rocket-launch year. But make it possible for your people to hit their bonuses if they work hard. We had one year where the entire industry was down, and our revenue goal for that year included growth over the previous year that was on pace with the growth we had been achieving. Well, the entire industry had an off year, and we didn't come close.

The next year, I set the goal at a level that was higher than anything we had ever done before, but our pace at the time I set the goal indicated we would blow past it. As a team, you have to have the accomplishment of achieving goals—that is every bit as important as the money. We did blow past the goal and would have succeeded at an even higher goal, but I wanted to be sure they had a win in this year.

A good portion of our incentive plan is based on team goals and a smaller portion on individual goals. I want everyone working together, and if one person with a client in town has a conflict, I need others to jump in and help without fearing that their production and bonus will suffer. This has worked very well for our team, and I see other companies that have individual-heavy bonus plans falling right into the traps that I am working to avoid.

I also provide a lot of intangibles that contribute to our high retention levels and employee engagement. I love a spontaneous party when we knock something out of the park. Call everyone in to the conference room at 10:00 a.m. and break out the wine and cheese! Team celebrations of all form and fashion are the norm—to the point where we sometimes struggle to come up with something new and out of the box to surprise everyone with. Flexible working hours and days off are imperative. I don't track days off or closely track vacation. Everyone puts in a lot of hours when we are busy. When we have a break in the action, I say please take advantage of it.

"The Thing Is, Nobody Wants to Disappoint You"

Peter Drucker said, "Culture eats strategy for lunch." People buy into strategy; they *live* culture. Every company creates their culture differently (unlimited Skittles, anyone?), but what high-performing companies have in common is a culture that people engage with beyond the core purpose of the business. Once again, this is not just a Millennial thing; people of all age groups need it. One of my team members once told me, "The thing is, nobody wants to disappoint you." I considered that the highest compliment. That means I have created an environment built around our unique culture, and not around rules, regulations, and seemingly irrelevant metrics.

• • •

Since so much of our business is focused on the human aspect of our events—some would call it the touchy-feely side—there has not been a lot of innovation in our industry over the years. Some venues may incorporate some impressive high-tech aspects, and some entertainers come up with cool things for the moment. But in the end, these tend toward being short-term trends that haven't shown a great deal of staying power. Marketing materials have become prettier, but little of substance has changed in twenty-five years.

I believe firmly that you must stay ahead of the curve in innovation or somebody will pass you by. Steve Jobs was known for insisting on pressing for new technology that went well beyond what customers expected. He always said that his customers didn't know yet what they wanted—just like when Henry Ford said that if you had asked his customers what they wanted, they would have said faster horses.

So I have pushed my team to come up with technologies that truly differentiate us from our competitors. My belief is that when a client sees something truly innovative, even if they don't need that particular innovation, it will position us as the smartest one in the room, and that will tilt the scales in our favor in the future.

Many years back, we created a video library of all our events, restaurants, and experiences. It consists of one-minute clips set to music that take you inside an event to meet the people who are making it happen. The clips are all professionally shot and edited, which was a very expensive endeavor. We update it regularly with new offerings. Our competitors generally have a video or two on their website, but nothing to the extent of what we have. Even within AlliedPRA, no other office has allocated the time and undertaken the expense to put something similar together. So we have a substantial competitive moat, and we have won numerous clients as a result of it.

One day we were discussing a transportation job and someone said, "Wouldn't it be great if we could see all of our vehicles on a smartphone app?" That would be a huge help to both our on-the-ground staff and our clients. The traditional system was antiquated: If a client needed to know where a sedan or a bus was, they called us; then we called the transportation company's dispatch offices, who looked up the GPS coordinates of the vehicle. Then we relayed the information back to the client as to where the vehicle was located and how long until we expected it at the destination. This could easily take five to ten minutes, depending on how busy everybody was.

I presumed that surely somebody had automated this process, and all we had to do was buy some software. How wrong I was! We looked everywhere and couldn't find off-the-shelf technology to do what we were looking for. It turns out that transportation is a particularly stodgy industry. To complicate things further, just within the twenty AlliedPRA offices that I surveyed, there were thirty different GPS systems operating in their preferred supplier companies. Stodgy and fragmented! Needless to say, none of the systems had the ability to interface with each other. By the time I was fully convinced that there was no solution out there, I was so far down the road on this idea mentally that I had to come up with a solution. What a road that turned out to be.

I figured we would hire a developer, pull some interfaces together, and be off and running. Of course, with technology it is never simple. First of all, I had a hard time finding someone to give us a fixed price on the development. Most companies gave an hourly rate and a vast, open-ended range of what it could turn out to be: essentially, a blank check once we contracted with them. I'm not comfortable with that scenario. We eventually hired a local developer with a reasonable fixed price, and he was able to get the foundation of the platform built. But he was not a good fit to grow the system long term, so we had to pivot midstream and almost start from scratch. I am happy to say that Neal Sus and the team at Susco have been great partners and have executed everything on time and on budget.

In the midst of kicking off the development, I was having a bar conversation with a friend who is a patent attorney.[10] I wondered if this

---

10 You might be amazed at how much work gets done at your local bar. Among the regulars at mine is a notary, and when I need something notarized, I just let him know to bring his stamp with him. I have arranged to have antique furniture reupholstered, received medical advice that led to the diagnosis of a hernia, had marketing consulting sessions with a great sales leader, swapped numerous tickets to sporting events, and, of course, all the rest of the betting and solving of the world's problems that go along with a diverse and charismatic crowd.

technology was worthy of a patent. Of course, always looking to drum up business, he was very encouraging. I soon discovered, though, that filing for a United States patent is a daunting process. The level of detail required to document your innovation and work around any potentially competing "prior art" is extensive. I had hours of excruciatingly detailed calls with our patent attorneys, and I must say it would have been a lot worse if not for the hand-holding by the team at Intellectual Property Consulting. Greg Latham, Kent Barnett, and their whole team did a great job of dumbing down the process for me. It took over a year to get the application filed and in front of a reviewer. We were confident there was not anything that had been previously filed that would get in our way. But the initial reviewer rejected us, citing a previous patent—owned by none other than Apple! Surely I couldn't compete with that. All the work seemed for naught. But as it turned out, Apple's patent was on a much narrower scope of application, and the IPC team was able to show the reviewer the case, and I am now the owner of United States Patent number 9,483,942 B2. That process is not for the faint of heart, but the ultimate success means that none of my competitors can ever claim that they provide a similar service. Another moat!

I continue to push for new and innovative ways to market our business, to provide new services, and to separate ourselves in the marketplace. This usually comes with a cost, and not everything I have tried has worked out. I try to find out quickly if an idea is worth pursuing before too much time and money gets spent on it. And I definitely have a dustbin of failed ideas. It's all about pushing forward and not being afraid of being wrong or failing.

From 2013 to 2016, year over year, our revenue grew in excess of fifty percent per year. Perhaps not a large number compared to venture capital–backed Silicon Valley start-ups, but in an industry that has not experienced significant growth, this was notable. The pie was not growing, so our high level of growth meant that we were taking market share from our competitors—which is much harder to do than throwing VC money at the Internet! At the same time, we were refining our pricing and our expense management, so the bottom line was growing as fast as the top (another thing the Silicon Valley folks who get all the press rarely do). We had built a solid team who were all outperforming their peer groups, and after all of the setbacks, we were in better shape than at any other time in the history of the company. It was only a matter of time before people were going to start to take notice.

CHAPTER TWELVE

OPEN FOR BUSINESS: LESSONS FROM KEY MOMENTS

"Success is the result of perfection, hard work, learning from failure, loyalty, and persistence."

—COLIN POWELL

This is a good place to take a break from the narrative and have a look at some leadership lessons I haven't covered up until now. These key factors are important to being successful in any small or start-up business, and they easily can be translated to other businesses and industries.

To begin, if I had to name the handful of traits that have been instrumental in getting me and my company to this point in our success, I would point to three—persistence, charm, and *cajones.*

Persistence

Because there are so many obstacles to growing a business, both expected and unexpected, it is easy to give up. In fact, the vast majority of people *do* give up. You have to fight your way through nonbelievers, failed strategies, and obstacles that come out of nowhere. You have to present your public face to motivate your team *and* your customers, and you have to keep it on your mind twenty-four hours a day. I think if you ask any entrepreneur what their most important trait is, persistence will rank number one the vast majority of the time.

Charm

You need people to believe in *you*. Team members, clients, and the people you owe money to—they all have to believe in you and your business—and stick with you. Don't be a bullshitter. Nobody likes one, and they are easy to see from a mile away. Everybody has different sources and types of charm. But whatever positive traits you have that people find attractive or unique, understand them, and use them. In my case, a bit of Irish charm is a nice finishing touch.

Cajones

That word speaks for itself. Being an entrepreneur is all about risks. It's not for the faint of heart. You can't be afraid of taking risks, but of course, you have to be calculated in the ones you choose. Don't take stupid ones, but remember: Nobody becomes wildly successful taking the safe route. You just have to buck up and stare your demons down—and you'll have to do it over and over.

People ask me at what point I will consider myself successful. I don't really know—I guess I will know it when I get there. A lot of people measure success in dollars, but money can go away tomorrow—often as a result of things outside your control. So that is not a great measure. Richard Branson is successful by any measure. Sam Zell is as well. Not just because of the wealth they have generated, but for what they have enabled the people in their organizations to do and become.

I respect most the people who have become wildly successful after starting with nothing or next to nothing. People who inherited their wealth and people who made money from their connections to government—not so much. While there is no question that it's never easy to become successful, starting with a huge advantage just doesn't resonate with me.

My Definition of Success

Here's what I do consider success to be: when I see a person make something of themselves as a result of an action I have put in place or a decision I have made. That success will last longer than any financial rewards ever can.

I *hate* turnover. It is expensive and disruptive. But sometimes people have to move along for reasons out of my control—as long as it is not to a competitor! Thankfully, none of my employees ever left me for a competitor. For those who did leave, I hope that I have set them up for success for the rest of their careers. The notes I've received from former team members over the years thanking me for providing the foundation for their successful careers mean more to me than any monetary achievements.

Remember Kim, who came in on twelve hours' notice and ran the BP operation at the Crowne Plaza for five months? She became our go-to person for all transportation staffing after that, and she began to build a team she liked working with. She developed enough of a roster that we just let her take over all the staffing for our transportation programs. She got to work with her hand-selected team and it saved us a lot of time. She started doing the same work for another DMC and a transportation company and turned those efforts into a successful staffing company that she now owns and operates. She used to be one of the first ones looking for her paycheck when an event ended; she is now a successful business owner.

Christie Drury, who also was crucial to our BP operation's success, joined us full time and became a rock-star sales manager. During that time, her father was paralyzed in a tree-cutting accident and suffered a number of setbacks related to the accident. Christie had become key to our operation—booking over one million dollars a year in sales. But she came to me one day and said that her dad couldn't run the beach volleyball complex any longer, and she would have to leave us to take over his company. At Coconut Beach, she has succeeded in modernizing the operation and building up group business, while bringing in new sponsors—she even landed an Olympic qualifying tournament. We get together regularly to talk business and exchange ideas, and when she brings up experiences that tie her current success back to her time at AlliedPRA, those are really fulfilling moments for me.

When Christie left, I was suddenly facing the potential of a one-million-dollar hole in sales production. That is freaking scary. However, as I've said, the way I run the business is to give everyone as much responsibility and as many challenges as I think they can handle. Note that I *don't* give them the responsibility and challenges that *they* think they can handle. A lot of times, I make people uncomfortable with the added challenges I may give them, but I always reinforce the fact that I believe they are up to the task. And when they inevitably succeed, we celebrate the success, and I remind them that they achieved something they didn't see that they could.

Erin Gremillion had taken on everything we had put in front of her and quickly moved up in the organization. Yet she was quietly playing a strong behind-the-scenes role to Christie and the rest of the sales team. When Christie left, Erin was the clear internal candidate to step into her role, but I was still shaking over the potential one-million-dollar loss. As it turned out, I needn't have worried. Erin quickly blew past a million dollars in her first year in the role and now confirms multiple times that amount. Set people up for success, turn them loose, and great things happen.

Always have a solid bench. You never know what is going to happen, and people are the most valuable resource in any business. The people who are not the stars of the show at the moment have to be ready to take on the role if one of the stars gets sidelined.

Invest in Your Team: Everyone Has Something to Give

I would much rather develop people internally than hire from the outside. One challenge in a small business is that it's natural for people to believe they can only go so far. I don't believe this is true. I encourage people to go after things that are of interest to them, even if it is outside our core business. Don't think only about the current structure: I will happily create new positions and new roles if we come up with a new opportunity.

Another thing about hiring from outside is that you pick up someone else's dirty laundry more often than not. Sometimes an outside hire is the only choice, as in when I brought in a Director of Sales. But my first preference is to take a young person and develop them.

Developing your team means investing in them. I mean this both financially and with time. Many small businesses don't dedicate the resources to continuing education. We do. We support our people with registration fees and the time off to attend a seminar in the area. If there is plane travel involved, we ask them to develop a list of expected takeaways from the conference to justify the investment. I also encourage them to attend seminars and events that are not related to our business, should they find something that interests them. Broadening one's range both in new knowledge and new contacts can only be helpful.

One year, we had our AlliedPRA company-wide annual meeting, but I didn't think the content was great or that we had gone down any new paths. Shortly thereafter I was in a session given by Jill Harrington at the SITE (Society for Incentive Travel Excellence) annual meeting in Panama. I thought, *This is just the training our team needs.* Jill spoke about maintaining relevance to your clients, turning the price conversation around, and overcoming obstacles in the sales process—exactly the shot in the arm my team needed.[11] Now, bringing in an internationally known speaker to speak to my small sales staff is expensive, and most people just wouldn't do it. So I decided to think even bigger, and I invited a number of our hotel partners from mid-size hotels that don't have big internal training budgets. It's important for me to be a valuable resource for our hotel partners (and not just ask them for referrals). We need referrals, too, of course, but if we can provide them with something extra, like opportunities to develop their careers, we are more likely to be top of mind when a client asks them for a referral for a DMC.

Supporting your team's efforts to get involved with industry organizations

---

11 Jill's book *Uncommon Sense: Shift Your Thinking. Take New Action. Boost Your Sales,* is a fantastic sales tool and is required reading for everyone in AlliedPRA.

is important as well. In a small business, you want to get as much outside-of-the-room perspective as possible, and this is a great way to do that.

I was giving a talk recently when one of the audience members asked how we ensure diversity in our company. I thought this was rather ironic, given that the slide that was visible of my team showed that I am clearly the only male in the group. I suppose I would need to hire more men if I wanted to ensure diversity! I don't think that is where the questioner was heading, though. My view is that in order for a company to be successful, you have to have a diversity of ideas, and this comes from including people with varying backgrounds and experiences. Many times, this naturally leads to people of different ethnicities, genders, and sexual orientations. But not exclusively. I have had hundreds of conversations with conservative, gay friends and rarely if ever disagreed on anything. Likewise with black business leader friends.

Just because someone is different in one of the defined categories does not mean you are adding diversity. On the flip side, a white male with a very different background, viewpoints, and outlook could provide exactly the diversity needed to grow the team. Society and so-called political correctness have become so obsessed with the issue of diversity and ensuring protected classes that it has become impossible to have a dialogue. If you are not on the side of the entitlement issue, you are automatically a racist and can't contribute to the conversation. In fact, several prominent academics and media people have come out lately to say that white men are inherently racist. If that is not a racist comment, I don't know what is! But somehow these people continue to get a platform.

The founders of a company are often going to be of a similar profile, because they are most likely to be within each other's trusted circle of people. But once you get past the founders, it is critical to have a diversity of backgrounds and perspectives in order to uncover the opportunities to grow the business. Let's just not get too hung up on what color they are or who they sleep with. That is reverse discrimination and goes exactly against the concept of everyone having an equal chance that we as a society are supposedly striving toward.

Every company has a number of stakeholders—in our case, the major categories are clients, hoteliers, suppliers, the franchise system, and shareholders. Your interaction with each of them has to contain messaging that is specific to each set of stakeholders. A broad explanation of why you are perfect for clients may not resonate with hoteliers. For years we used similar messaging for all categories of stakeholders: We provide great service and we are creative and innovative. But what you really have to do is dig into each relationship to determine what is useful to the people you are in front of at the moment.

For clients, all of these things may resonate, but some may be more important than others. Focus on which of your key selling points are important to that particular client, and drill down on those rather than giving a laundry list of all your attributes. To our suppliers, service is an important message, because we rely on them so we all can provide great service to our clients. But creativity and innovation may not be so important to suppliers. What is important to them is having a fair partnership and getting paid on time. To hoteliers, service is important, but most important is how we can make their job easier and provide tools that allow them to increase sales.

A FEW MORE RANDOM LESSONS FROM TWENTY-PLUS YEARS OF ENTREPRENEURSHIP

- *Always* do everything that is public-facing first class—even when you don't have the money. Your reputation and your brand are what will drive success for you. Your public image is a big part of that.

- Don't be so caught up in your business that you neglect the rest of your life. Make time to enjoy the fruits of your labors. I have traveled the world, been on all seven continents, seen some amazing places, and, more important, met some incredible people. I have a solid financial plan going forward, but the ultimate success will be that when I die, the last check bounces.

continued

- When you are in a conversation with someone, make that person feel special. Bobby Bowden, the retired Florida State football coach, meets hundreds of people a day. But each time I have met him and introduced myself, he has said, "Jeff, it is great to see you. How are you doing?" or something similar. During the few minutes he spends talking to you, he is fully engaged and sincerely interested in *you*, and he makes you feel like you are the only important person in his world at that moment. It is a lesson in class and communication, and it is one reason he has been so successful with recruiting, with alumni relations, and with his team. You are in the conversation anyway—make every one count.

- The most valuable asset you have is *time*. It is the only thing that is not replaceable. I have been broke more times than I can count and came back. Lost everything I owned—twice. Lost loves, but new ones came along. The only thing you cannot get back once it is lost is time, so invest your time with the preciousness it deserves. Hold your schedule to this standard: The things you do should advance you toward your goals, be they personal or professional. And resist people who abuse your time. Which leads me to . . .

- Don't be late. I *hate* being late. Nothing shows disrespect to the person you are meeting more than not being on time and, therefore, depriving them of that irreplaceable asset. I am insistent on not doing it to others, and if you do it to me, it *will* be remembered. What kind of message are you sending to someone you want to do business with if you can't even organize yourself to be on time?

- Do the hard stuff first. This is also known as "eating the frog." If you tackle the hardest tasks in front of you first, you will have created an accomplishment, and that will make the rest of what you need to do seem easy. This is based on a quotation attributed to Mark Twain: "Eat a live frog first thing in the morning and nothing worse will happen to you the rest of the day." So don't procrastinate—eat the frog!

- Ace Greenberg was CEO of Bear Stearns from 1978 to 1993 and chairman of the board from 1985 to 2001. He was notorious for his memos to his staff, and his book *Memos from the Chairman* is a hilariously good lesson in business. One thing that sticks out in my mind is his obsession with paper clips. He refused to approve any purchases of paper clips, reasoning that the company received so many paper clips in the mail with the correspondence they received that if they just removed them before throwing things in the trash, they should never have to buy a paper clip. A small thing, sure, but a free way to improve your margin. I *never* waste a paper clip, as a result.

- Look after your health! I should do a better job of practicing what I preach here. I do get to the gym several times a week, get the proper amount of sleep, and stay active with outdoor pursuits. But I could still drop some weight. Goodness knows, I am trying. Staying healthy and in good physical shape is key to making your brain work better.

• • •

Today's company founders certainly face a different environment than I did when I started my first business. So much has shifted to e-commerce, social media plays a huge part in promoting your business, and the needs and expectations of customers change much more quickly. The amount of information that is out there about your company and everyone else is vast, which can be helpful, and it can be a danger. But don't ever lose sight of the importance of personal relationships, both inside and outside your organization. You need a great team, great relationships with your investors, and great relationships with your customers, even if they're not face-to-face relationships. You can't hide behind a screen and have effective relationships. I hope I've made it clear throughout these chapters how this has contributed significantly to my success. The greatest product in the world goes nowhere without all of the stakeholders—who are all humans with thoughts, needs, and emotions—being committed to it.

CHAPTER THIRTEEN

MAKING IT TO THE INC. 5000

"There are no traffic jams along the extra mile."

—ROGER STAUBACH

On July 14, 2016, AlliedPRA New Orleans was named to the Inc. 5000 list of the fastest-growing, privately-held companies in the United States. This first-time honor was a particularly proud moment for me because of all it took to get to that point, and it made me think about all of the events and people that led to this.

Being an entrepreneur is a roller coaster in so many ways. You never know what is coming next around the corner, and the uncertainty of it all provides the excitement that I thrive on. It is so much fun if you are lucky enough to get your thrills this way.

If you are an entrepreneur reading this book, you surely have been doing a lot of nodding at what I have had to say. If you are not, it may not resonate, because your entrepreneur friends likely don't tell you about their trials and tribulations. While it is a journey that many people become a part of, the gory details are usually stomached alone. As the entrepreneur, you have to be the driving force of the business, getting the team's buy-in while telling customers and the media what a great story and product you have. Meanwhile, behind the scenes, you are trying to figure out how to make payroll. You just don't tell people that, because they will lose faith, and in a new business, faith is all you are selling.

So most entrepreneurs are left to handle the headaches and heartaches of building a business internally. Unfortunately, many times this swings over into their personal lives. Divorces are common; so are bankruptcies. When advising new or aspiring entrepreneurs, I always counsel them to be brutally honest with their spouse about the potential downsides. Mortgage payments will be late and bills will be juggled while the family finances swing on the fortunes of the business. It is best to have your spouse fully prepared from the beginning.

There is an old adage that says what you do when nobody is watching defines your character. This is so true, and it speaks to the ethics and unselfishness that is required to make you successful. I have pointed out a few people in this book who did not live this, and karma got each of them. The added truth as a business owner is that it is rare that nobody is watching. *Everybody* is watching, all the time—particularly when you are pre-product or pre-revenue. Investors, clients, your team—they are all always on alert for the smallest indication of what direction you and the business are going. Knowing that means you are on alert twenty-four hours a day, always conscious of yourself and the business. Twenty years into this, I still feel the same way. It can lead to a lot of stress, which, again, ends up being internalized.

On the issue of internalization, do note that there are a number of organizations that form a sort of support group for entrepreneurs to address that exact issue. I know many entrepreneurs who swear by them and have reaped great rewards personally, both emotionally and by growing their network. I have been involved with several, but for me it always seems like a lot of navel-gazing, with the conversations dominated by a few people who have small problems, or personal ones. I don't find the value in it. I'd rather blow off steam to Sam and Shane at the bar. But that's me. As I said, lots of people find benefits from these organizations, so they may be right for you.

In the course of building the business, I refinanced my house fully, twice, and on a third occasion, I took out a substantial home equity loan. All of the proceeds went into the business. In theory, my partner should have been on the hook for half of the company's cash needs, but he had a wife and kids and financial issues of his own. His wife was certainly not going to let him refinance their house. I sold one of the B&Bs for a substantial profit, and I plowed all that money into the business as well. Before I knew it, I had loaned almost a half-million dollars to the company. When Katrina hit, it looked like I might never get that back. More recently, we got into a situation where we had over $600,000 in accounts receivable—money people owed us for work we had already done. The balance sheet looked great, but the bank account was empty. I sold my Apple stock at $117 to make payroll and within weeks it shot up to $160; missed out on a huge gain. But that is what you have to do to keep the business running. There is never a magic bailout coming.

In a new business, cash flow is always a problem. You are spending money faster than you are making it and getting paid for your work well after the work is done. It is critical to keep your eye on the horizon and plan for coming swings in cash flow—they will *always* come—and put a plan in place before it becomes a crisis. Your options are fewer and more expensive once it becomes a crisis. Don't make the mistake of waiting until you are knee-deep in the problem before trying to do something about it. It's a rookie mistake.

Vivian and I have been together over ten years now, and I can't emphasize enough how much having a stable and supportive partner at home helps make running the business easier. In my earlier years, I had a penchant for bodacious, bombastic, high-energy, big-personality women. Fun times for sure, but the drama that goes along with the type-AAA personality can cause a lot of stress, and even if it didn't carry over outwardly, it would get internalized, fighting with all of the other stresses that business owners have to internalize.

Vivian is beautiful, smart, patient, and caring. She has a wonderful family who took me in from the start and who have been an amazing part of my life. And they are Greek, so you know the food is out of this world!

My job consists of a lot of travel to meet clients, and when I am home, often I am out to dinner with clients or at industry events. Fortunately, Vivian was in this business previously, so she understands the demands. It is never an issue when I can't be home for dinner or if I have to hit the road for a client meeting or a trade show. She is never concerned about the fact that I am often the only straight guy in a room full of women—it is an occupational hazard. Where some women would have seen constant threats, she understands the dynamic and understands that I simply see a lot of great professionals on a daily basis. She is always ready with a smile at the end of a long day or a long trip. When she has to be the plus-one at an event where she doesn't know anybody, she just makes friends and has a good time. Lesser spouses are pulling at your elbow to leave from the minute you walk in the door. For those of you who have a spouse like Vivian, you are truly blessed. For those whose spouse falls into the former category, I feel your pain. I am lucky, blessed, and profoundly appreciative.

• • •

In the midst of the aftereffects of 9/11, Katrina, and the Great Recession, I was not thinking about making the Inc. 5000; I wasn't even thinking about breaking even. It was pure survival mode. But survive we did, and all of the persistence, charm, and cajones ultimately paid off with that handsome recognition. I always knew we could do it, but there were many times when the outlook was bleaker than others. But not considering failure as an option, I pressed ahead and brought my partners and team along for the ride.

Being honored as a member of the Inc. 5000 was, to me, more than just a recognition of a successful year. It was a culmination of having overcome all of the challenges that it takes to create a successful business over twenty years of hard work, determination, and persistence in the face of some seemingly insurmountable obstacles.

The following year, we were once again named to the Inc. 5000. The notification letter indicated that less than one in three Inc. 5000 recipients receive the award again. It is an honor for fast growth—something that is by definition hard to maintain. At the same time, we were named to the inaugural Seminole 100. This is a recognition from the Jim Moran Institute for Global Entrepreneurship at Florida State University. It is recognition of the 100 fastest-growing companies owned by Florida State alumni. We were number thirty-eight. It was particularly special and fulfilling to get this honor from my alma mater, which I so dearly love. Go Noles!

Jim Moran grew up of modest means in Chicago. The entrepreneurial bug caught him early, largely out of necessity to help support his mother. He owned several car dealerships in Chicago before moving to Florida and starting Southeast Toyota. JM Family Enterprises is now one of the largest companies in the automotive industry (and coincidentally, a great client of AlliedPRA New Orleans!). The director of the institute was giving Vivian and me a tour of the facility during the celebration weekend, and she shared a great story that sums up Jim's simple genius. In the early days of his dealerships in Florida, Jim would offer a free quart of ice cream to anyone who test-drove one of his cars. Well, it was hot in Florida, and refrigeration systems were not what they are today, so Jim knew that they would have to go straight home and eat the ice cream and wouldn't be able to go to one of his competitors to test-drive their cars! I love innovative marketing stories, and some of the simplest ones are the most successful.

As a result of both of these honors, I have met a lot of interesting people. James Barlow of Blue Air Training is one of them. His company was number one on the inaugural Seminole 100. A retired fighter pilot, he has acquired mothballed fighter jets from foreign governments like Jordan, Ecuador, and New Zealand, to name a few. He refurbished them and developed a team to provide close-air combat training to our military (and is about to expand to other countries). My banker has financed a number of projects for me over the years fairly willingly, but I can only imagine the response I would get if I went to him and said, "Bob, I need fourteen million dollars to buy a fighter jet from Ecuador!"

I mentioned to James that there probably was not a lot of competition in his marketplace, and his response was that they are the only company licensed by the Department of Defense to do what they do. His serious demeanor cracked with a wry smile when telling me this. Talk about a moat! The point is, when you get outside of your normal industry circle, you meet some unique people and gain new perspectives. I love doing this, and I always come back with new ideas for my business.

• • •

I rarely get too up or too down. Twenty years of entrepreneurship have taught me that whatever the cause of the current high or low—it can all reverse itself tomorrow. But in the case of these honors, I was truly excited. After all the years of challenges, setbacks, and internalizing all of the issues, we were being recognized publicly for our success. I was happy for myself, but more so, I was really proud of the team's accomplishment. A band of industry rookies joined the team one by one, bought into the vision, and produced results well beyond expectations.

CHAPTER FOURTEEN

WHAT A LONG STRANGE TRIP . . .

"You miss 100 percent of the shots you don't take."

—WAYNE GRETZKY

E arly in my career I thought I was going to be a hotel mogul—first with Sheraton and then with my growing chain of B&Bs. But the winds changed, and I ended up going in a different direction. Along the way, there were too many pivots to count, but you have to adjust the sails when the wind changes direction.

Living out of my car as a teenager, losing everything I owned twice, the business setbacks of 9/11, Katrina, and the Great Recession—I've overcome my share of things. There is nothing you can do to change the past, so looking ahead for the next opportunity has always been my mind-set. I could only control what was in front of me, and as long as I had beer money, I figured I could make it to the next place (a big thank-you to Vic LaBorde at Fat Harry's for extending credit when the beer money was a little tight!).

I've always tried different combinations of things until I hit on a winning formula. Every day, I spend a little bit of time looking for new innovations that we can make in the DMC business and looking around for new opportunities outside the DMC business. I don't have a preconceived notion of what these opportunities may be, but I am always looking.

Through it all, the inherent traits I had—of persistence, charm, and cajones—have served me well. Some of those traits are surely genetic, but knowing nothing about my biological parents, I'm not sure whom

I should thank for them. I am certain that my parents were both very successful people if what they have given me is any indication. The balance of my life is a product of my environment. Life throws curveballs, and as I mentioned before, it ain't for sissies. Looking for the good and the opportunity—no matter how small, in any setback—focuses you on what can be done going forward rather than what has already happened. I tell people all the time, "You can't change the past; you can only change the future."

I was doing an interview recently about the effects of Katrina and the Recession, and the writer asked me if there was ever a time when I felt that it was all not going to work out. I know she was looking for some dramatic moment of despair, so I thought about it carefully to be sure I was giving her a good answer. But after digging deep, I could truthfully say no. Throughout it all, I felt that if I kept pressing ahead, good things would happen.

For all of the challenges, headaches, and heartaches of being an entrepreneur, it is, above and beyond everything else, a lot of fun. The high that comes along with a big sales success is multiplied by a hundred when it is in your own business. Developing people so that they can have successful careers is the greatest feeling in the world. So is the bond you've developed with your team that makes them want to make you proud of their successes. All of these things continue to become much more personal and much more meaningful in a company you've built yourself.

I am particularly proud of the long line of industry stars who have developed on my watch. Courtney Fields is the latest in that line and now is our top Event Producer. Small in stature but big in personality, she has a flair for creativity that results in the most amazing events. Her tenacious attitude pushes our suppliers to come up with better and better events, and it keeps everybody in line at the same time. Watching her events come together is a master class in organization and precision.

Our team has won numerous industry awards, and we have had the highest client satisfaction scores in all of AlliedPRA—five times. Erin Gremillion was named Hospitality Industry Millennial of the Year in New

Orleans. All of our stars hold leadership positions in industry and local organizations and sit on boards of directors and lead committees.

The other companies I have founded have taught me important lessons as well. Having three B&Bs with $25,000 worth of monthly mortgage payments when 9/11 hit has given me a great aversion to debt. I know there will come a time when I again will have to lever up a company in order to take it to the next level, but I will be very convinced of the outcome before doing so.

Taking advantage of big hotel chains' slowness to adapt in the advent of the Internet age was an interesting glimpse into the mind-set of big companies. It translated into how we look at investments in start-up companies (more on that to follow). Several of my investing partners have worked for big conglomerates, and they regularly remind us that big companies are not able to pivot quickly in the marketplace, which opens doors for opportunistic small companies to step in. Having experienced this firsthand, I know that is the case.

It was certainly never in my life's plan to open a hotel in Bunkie, Louisiana. But I had positioned myself as an expert in the marketplace when it came to historic renovations and small hotels. When the need came up, somebody thought of me, and I was able to move on the opportunity quickly and make it happen. (Postscript on that one: The owners treated the property more like a personal playground than a business, and it eventually folded. I had long since completed my contractual obligations and moved along, better for the experience in spite of the squirrels.)

Starting the Avis car rental business was not in the plan either. It was born out of necessity. The Recession was taking a toll on AlliedPRA, and we needed to diversify our revenue stream. Frankly, we didn't know anything about the car rental business going into it. But we did our research and presented a solid plan to the people at Avis, and they bought into it. Before long, we were leading all of the Agency Operators in the region in all of the key operational metrics and generating healthy cash flow. It was one of the many times I have had to pivot to adjust to a circumstance or opportunity. Don't ever think everything is written in stone!

2018 and Beyond

The year 2017 was an off year—both for us and the industry as a whole. All of the cities in the AlliedPRA portfolio underperformed relative to the previous year, and all the hotels in New Orleans shared a similar story. There doesn't seem to be any concrete explanation for it. The best explanation that has gathered some concurrence is that the uncertainty of the election of 2016 delayed companies' decision making. Not the result itself, just the uncertainty of the outcome. If Hillary Clinton had been elected, her unfriendly business policies would have caused problems for a lot of industries. If Donald Trump were to get elected— well, nobody knew what to expect there. As such, it seems that during the critical fall booking season, a lot of companies sat on their hands and waited out the election rather than committing investment for 2017 meetings and events.

As a result, in 2017 we did over a million dollars less in revenue and posted a solid loss. Fortunately, we already had a good base developing for 2018, so there was no need to panic. Rather than cut back, we continued to invest in education, marketing, and sales trips, the same as if we were having a normal year. I didn't want to lose any momentum, so I self-financed the losses. That decision would pay off in spades in 2018.

• • •

Another storyline was playing out as 2017 turned toward 2018. Terry and I had been business partners for almost twenty years as 2017 came to a close. After we exited the Avis business, we bought some residential rental real estate and acquired the Property Management Inc. franchise for the New Orleans area. Our first full year of the PMI business was far from projections, in part due to a longer-than-expected booking process in the residential property management market and in part because of some moves that Terry made that were counter to what I had advocated for.

I came to the realization that the best way to make that business successful would be to give it a cash infusion and to give Terry the autonomy to do things the way he wanted. Just before Christmas 2017, we agreed to end the partnership. I bought him out of his interest in AlliedPRA, providing the cash for the runway he needed to build PMI. He kept the PMI business, and I kept a complex of apartments we had acquired. It was one of the toughest things I have ever had to do, and frankly, we had probably put it off longer than we should have. But it was a stress relief for me to not have the other business to support, and it gave Terry the money and autonomy to run his company.

• • •

In the past few years I have also become active in investing in start-up companies. My portfolio to date includes a wind energy development in Nebraska, a cybersecurity company, a babysitting app, a classic watch company, a company making "nerve on a chip" technology for pharmaceutical testing, a specialty watch company, a hotel in the Bakken oil fields, and a few others.

Here are brief profiles of each. Perhaps by the time you read this, one of these companies will have hit it large.

- Aksamit Resource Management—Wind energy development in south central Nebraska

- Mainstay Suites Stanley—Extended-stay hotel in the Bakken oil region of North Dakota

- Swimlane—Cybersecurity automation platform, based in Denver

- Sitter—The "Uber of Babysitting" app, based in Boulder

- Vortic Watch Company—A small-batch custom watch manufacturing and vintage restoration company, based in Fort Collins

- AxoSim—Nerve-on-a-Chip platform for pharmaceutical testing, based in New Orleans

- Embera—Pharmaceutical products in pipeline to combat addiction, based in Boston

- Fluence Analytics—Industrial polymer monitoring equipment, based in New Orleans

- Mastery Prep—College admissions testing preparation company, based in Baton Rouge

- Microbiome Therapeutics—Health and nutrition products aimed at improving gastrointestinal health, based in New Orleans

- CurvaFix—Medical device company that has developed a device to improve outcomes of surgery for broken hips and pelvises, based in Seattle

As you see, it is a very diverse group of companies. I have invested in some of them due to personal relationships with the founders and others through angel investment groups that I belong to. Being a member of an angel investment group is a great way to get involved with early-stage company investing. For one thing, you get access to deal flow that an individual would not have. More important, the screening and due diligence process to vet the potential investments is much stronger and more robust than an individual can handle. You get the advantage of working with a lot of seasoned investors and entrepreneurs to dissect the opportunities and provide the information to help make your investment decisions. Even when you don't invest, you have the opportunity to see multiple pitches per month, which is interesting itself. I am an active member of Lagniappe Angels and NOLA Angel Network in New Orleans and Rockies Venture Club in Colorado.

I enjoy mentoring young entrepreneurs, both in my portfolio companies and outside of them. The excitement of someone with a new idea or a new company is contagious. Every successful entrepreneur has had a lot of great mentors and role models. Each of us should give back a multiple of what we have received in that vein. It is a small price to pay for the gifts that we have been given.

The great news is that at fifty-two I still have a long way to go. I have started ten companies in the last twenty years, so who knows what the next twenty to thirty years will bring? The team at AlliedPRA is firing on all cylinders, which has given me the time to explore some new avenues—even as I am still day-to-day hands-on involved with running the company. I work remotely from my townhouse in Vail regularly, thanks to the patience of Vivian and the leadership in the office. Being outdoors in the mountains gives me a lot of fresh ideas and gives me the opportunity to get the exercise needed to stave off the aging process.

I am as excited for the next opportunity as I was when I started the first company over twenty years ago. When I walked out the door of the Sheraton New Orleans that May Monday in 1996, I had no idea what the next step would be, and I never would have predicted it would be all of this. But the journey has taught me that there is always some new challenge, opportunity, and excitement around the next corner. And more important, that it is impossible to predict what that will be. So always be ready to roll with the punches and ride whatever wave might be coming your way. It has turned out quite well for me.

What happens next is anybody's guess. I haven't put a whole lot of thought into it, other than I don't ever intend to stop working. Bobby Bowden once said, "After retirement, there is just one major event left, and I ain't looking forward to it." I couldn't agree with you more, Coach!

The challenge of starting and running businesses is just too much fun to ever slow down. My brain goes so stir-crazy over a three-day weekend, so there is no way I could sit around for weeks or months at a time—or eternity. The role models of business owners working into their eighties and nineties are numerous, and I expect to do the same. I'll presumably take on different roles than I have so far, but I'll be going after it just as hard nonetheless.

Ray Kroc started McDonald's in his fifties. Time is on my side. I don't know how the next thirty or forty years will play out, but it will be fun. And, of course, here's hoping the last check bounces . . .

ABOUT THE AUTHOR

Jeff O'Hara began his hospitality career in 1985 while working part time as a student at Florida State University. His career has taken him to every corner of the hospitality industry, from luxury boutique hotels and 1,000-plus-room "supertankers" to managing small restaurants and developing B&Bs.

Jeff moved to New Orleans in 1992 while he was with Sheraton Hotels for what he laughingly describes as "a two-year assignment"—the city has been his home ever since. Since 1997, his primary focus has been on Destination Management, for which he has a unique passion and which has allowed him to work with groups from around the country and around the globe.

Since purchasing the AlliedPRA New Orleans franchise in 2002, he has made the New Orleans destination experience his focus, winning numerous awards and accolades in the process. In 2016 and 2017, AlliedPRA was named to the Inc. 5000 fastest-growing private companies in America, and in 2017, it made the inaugural Seminole 100 list of fastest-growing companies owned by Florida State University alumni.

Along the way, Jeff started and developed seven other hospitality businesses and two real estate companies. He has backed several start-ups as an angel investor in the fields of technology, biotech, consumer staples, and alternative energy and has also backed start-ups through the Rockies Venture Club, NOLA Angel Network, and Lagniappe Angels.

A native of Kingston, New York, Jeff received a BS in Hospitality Administration from Florida State University and an MBA from Tulane University. He lives in New Orleans with his longtime partner, Vivian. His father lives in Upstate New York, and his sister and brother live in Fort Lauderdale, Florida, and Sioux Falls, South Dakota. Jeff devotes his leisure time to outdoor pursuits—skiing, golfing, hiking, biking, and fishing.